PLANTS & GARDENS

BROOKLYN BOTANIC GARDEN RECORD

Gardening for Wildlife

1987

Brooklyn Botanic Garden

Staff for this issue:

SALLY L. TAYLOR, *Guest Editor*

BARBARA B. PESCH, *Editor*

CHARLES GABELER, *Art Director*

JO KEIM, *Assistant Editor*

and the Editorial Committee of the Brooklyn Botanic Garden

DONALD E. MOORE, *President, Brooklyn Botanic Garden*

ELIZABETH SCHOLTZ, *Director Emeritus*

STEPHEN K-M. TIM, *Vice President, Science & Publications, Brooklyn Botanic Garden*

First printing, November 1987
Second printing, November 1988
ISBN 0-945352-45-X

PLANTS & GARDENS
BROOKLYN BOTANIC GARDEN RECORD

Gardening for Wildlife

Vol. 43   1987   No. 3

CONTENTS

Cover Photograph by Elvin McDonald
Mallards at Home

Plants and Gardens, Brooklyn Botanic Garden Record (ISSN 0362-5850) is published quarterly at 1000 Washington Ave., Brooklyn, N.Y. 11225, by the **Brooklyn Botanic Garden, Inc.** Second-class-postage paid at Brooklyn, N.Y., and at additional mailing offices. Subscription included in Botanic Garden membership dues ($20.00 per year), which includes newsletters, announcements and plant dividends.

foreword

In the course of assembling this handbook, I was amazed by the depth of feeling people have for the wildlife in their gardens. Not all the feelings are positive—one can hardly applaud the presence of deer sampling prized woody plantings. But today's garden community is more tolerant of garden wildlife overall as research reveals its benefits. Birds help control harmful insects, butterflies and bees are natural pollinators, and studies on the interaction between plant and animal offer new information in all sciences, including medicine.

The hazards from indiscriminately killing all insects with non-specific chemicals and effectively removing the "good guys" as well as the "bad guys" are a prime research concern. Integrated pest management programs which call for precise knowledge, and studies on life cycles of plant predators, are finally reducing dependence on these chemicals.

Knowledge of the intricacies of a plant's own chemical defenses against predators has opened a whole new world. It is now possible to consider the alteration of a plant's genetic makeup, endowing it with the ability to manufacture its own pesticide.

Our lives are enriched when we can learn to coexist in the natural world of our gardens.

SALLY TAYLOR

Pert black-capped chickadee visits feeder for sunflower seeds. These birds always add a note of cheer to the garden.

Garden with wattle fence, fruit trees, flowering plants, and grape vine. The usual fountain replaced by a statue on a pedestal. End of 15th Century.

6

An African-Roman Villa—a mosaic from the baths of Pompeianus

Wildlife in the Pleasure Garden

Sally Taylor

The very human attempt to attract and keep animals in garden-like settings is illustrated throughout history. From the earliest Egyptian tomb paintings depicting natural landscapes, animals have been shown. The flowering meadow of the medieval unicorn tapestries is populated with birds, rabbits, dogs and the mythical unicorn. The paradise gardens of Persia, the gardens of the Gods, the sacred groves of the Greeks and other such "pleasure gardens" are part of our cultural consciousness.

Marcus Terentius Varro (116-27BC), author of *Res Rusticae* described a Roman villa-garden with an aviary, or "ornithon." Additional features of the garden were fishponds and "hare-warrens," where rabbits were raised for the Roman market. Bees, snails, and birds were kept for both pleasure—'delectionis causa"—and profit. Varro describes, according to Thacker (1979), an outdoor aviary 18 by 72 feet, within which birds were confined by nets on either side of a dining area. While guests dined, birds sang for their pleasure.

Pliny the Younger (100 A.D.) describes frescoes of birds ornamenting the walls of his Tuscan villa, as well as a "hippodrome" or riding ground. Pliny the Elder wrote of a "verdant val-

Convent Garden of A.D. 1490, with raised banks running round the walls. Flowers are growing either in the beds or in pots placed upon them as well as on the ground.

Sally Lockett Taylor, guest editor of this handbook, is Associate Professor of Botany at Connecticut College and Director of the Human Ecology Program. She is the author of many papers and books and was guest editor of Plants and the Home Gardener, *a handbook published in 1984.*

Garden or Apiary surrounded and divided in two by a wattle fence.

ley," with a river flowing through the landscape and of the landscape "melodious with the choral songs of birds" (Thacker, 1979).

The nightingale was a favorite bird of Islamic gardens. It was paired in poetry with the rose, a flower native to the Middle East. Persian poets in the 12th century described soul-birds singing at the same time as roses opened, announcing spring; *praising the rose.* The rose bud was compared to the nightingale's heart. In Isfahan in 1598, Shah Abbas created a garden city with birds free or in aviaries amid closely planted trees.

Salomon de Caus, in *Raison des Forces Movantes,* written in 1615, describes the famous "owl and birds" statue of the Villa D'Este in Italy. During the 13th and 14th century in England, orchards with fishponds, aviaries and menageries were featured in the gardens of noblemen. Devices like talking owls and water surprises were constructed per directions given in the Arabic *Book of Mechanical Devices* written by al Jazari of Dyarbakir in 1206. The owl turns its head toward the birds, which stop singing, and when the owl looks away, the birds start to sing again. By cleverly using air and water pressure it was possible to imitate the songs of small birds. De Caus' brother, Isaac, designed at Wilton the first of the large formal gardens in England, with hunting parks, fishponds and aviaries.

Cattle and sheep became part of the extended landscape with the introduction of the ha-ha in the 1700s. A depressed ditch which animals could not cross, the ha-ha permitted large animals to be contained yet visible along the outer margins of the rustic landscape, thus replacing the walled gardens of an earlier era. In the gardens at Rousham, designed by William Kent in 1738, part and parcel of the landscape is a glorious dovecote, where birds nested. Eggs, birds and droppings were all useful to the farm operation and at the dinner table. It is today a working estate maintained as it was when the boundary wall between garden and field was breached.

In 1820 an octagonal Chinese aviary was constructed at Dropmore House, England. It had a raised dome where birds could fly freely. Humphry Repton, noted English garden designer, created a design for an aviary for the Royal Pavilion at Brighton in 1806.

In this century, Longleat was the first great English estate to return to keeping a menagerie as an income-earning device. One can visit the lions of Longleat, not to mention camels and monkeys as well. Here, too, Indian peacocks and peahens stroll the grounds uncaged. Also notable are the dolphin fountains of Chatsworth. Topiary animals of all descriptions still populate gardens in England and in the U.S. Topiary was perfected by the Romans; dolphin fountains were a feature of Renaissance gardens (as in the Villa Lante in Italy).

Old World civilizations did not originate the idea of animals in "gardens for pleasure." Hyams (1971) quotes Prescott's *History of the Conquest of Mexico* (1886), wherein is paraphrased a Spanish translation of an Aztec history, written by Iztlilxochitl. The palace garden of the Aztec king of Texcoco with its fountains, birds and fish is described.

. . . ."birdhouse where the King of Texcoco in Mexico kept animals, reptiles and serpents they brought him from every part of New Spain, either alive or figured in gold and gems."

Cortez described another royal garden as being watered by aqueducts, divided into sections, and having "in one quarter an aviary, filled with numerous kinds of birds remarkable in this region for brilliancy of plumage and song" (Hyams, 1971).

Here in the United States, William Randolph Hearst assembled a collection of exotic grazing animals (including zebra) for the rolling hills of his mountaintop castle, San Simeon, in California.

Pigeon feeding in St. Marks Square in Venice or near the great mosques in Istanbul, or in Central Park in New York City, is yet another extension of the human urge to have animals in the landscape. Whether in town or country, we can indeed attest to much of the feeling which stirred in our forebears for "wildlife" in the garden.

Bibliography

Fleming, Lawrence and Alan Gore. The English Garden. Michael Joseph Ltd., London. 1979.
Hyams, Edward. A History of Gardens and Gardening. Praeger Publishers, New York. 1971.
Thacker, Christopher. The History of Gardens. University of California Press, Berkeley. 1979.

Editor's note: The woodcuts illustrating this article were selected from histories of herbals in BBG's special library collections.

"Garden of Love," with railed benches, from Der Meister der Liebesgärten, *A.D. 1450.*

How To Landscape For Birds

Stephen W. Kress

North American wild bird populations are facing frightening losses of habitat. Factors contributing to this loss are: the drainage of wetlands, fragmentation of woodland nesting habitats and deforestation of tropical wintering habitat. Even habitats "protected" in parks and sanctuaries may be affected by inconspicuous changes resulting from acid rain, or the introduction of such competitive birds as European starlings and house sparrows.

While many environmental problems may seem beyond your ready action, there are things which you can do for birds that will, at the same time, improve your own property or your community's parks. In this article we'll consider some of the positive changes you can make to assist wild bird populations.

The number and variety of birds occupying your land is determined by limiting factors. These factors include food, water, cover, nest sites and singing posts. Parasites, diseases and predators may also limit populations, but are generally not as critical. By careful manipulation of food, cover, water and nest sites, you can greatly alter the population of birds on your property.

Sometimes simply putting up a birdhouse or adding a fresh water source will be enough to bring wild birds onto your land. Providing food at feeders however, is rarely enough action to induce year-round increases in bird populations. You must also consider cover, nest sites and water supplies.

Often, the kinds of plants and the way they grow are the most important limiting factors. By careful selection and arrangement of bird-attracting plants, you can substantially increase the number and variety of birds which visit your property. Here are a few guidelines to help in assessing your property's potential *and* things to keep in mind when arranging new habitats.

Consider "edges"

Studies of wild bird communities demonstrate that where there are abundant "edges" between habitats, there will also be a greater variety of birds. This is because edges offer a mix of different foods and shelter. For example, where a hedgerow joins open lawn, foods are present both in the plants of the lawn (i.e., *seed* from crabgrass, sheep sorrel and clover), and from the hedge (i.e., *fruit* from privet, pyracantha, elderberry or sumac).

Each habitat also has different kinds of insects and other invertebrates, providing greater variety to natural food supplies. Furthermore, each habitat also provides different amounts of roosting cover and nest sites.

There are also "micro-edges" within each habitat. Hedges, for example, may consist of several kinds of shrubs that produce fruit at different times of the year. Each of these will have a somewhat different height, stem structure, location of fruit and foliage shape. Wherever different shrubs come together in the same hedge, they create a "micro-edge" that further alters the food, cover and nesting potential of the hedge. For example, hedges which contain both deciduous and coniferous shrubs provide more varied roosting and nesting opportunities than hedges composed of only one type.

Stephen W. Kress is a staff biologist for the National Audubon Society and an Associate at the Laboratory of Ornithology. His book is The Audubon Society Guide to Attracting Birds, *published by Charles Scribner's Sons.*

Where there are abundant edges between habitats, there will be a greater variety of birds. This is because a selection of foods and shelter is provided. Shown at right is BBG's Local Flora section—a haven for both migrants and year-round residents.

Edges between habitats change in both horizontal and vertical direction, so its important to consider two planes when attempting to improve your yard for birds. A yard with mixed height plantings of close-cropped lawn, wildflowers, ground cover, shrubs and trees will have more edges and hence more birds. Conversely, expansive uniform habitats, whether close-cropped land, thicket or forest will have a paucity of birds.

Layer Your Property for More Vertical Edge

One reason tropical rainforests have so many kinds of birds is because they've a number of layers—running from ground to highest canopy. These forest layers are connected by vines and a tangle of vegetation growing from large tree trunks. Each layer is like a floor in a tall apartment building, complete with resident plants, insects, frogs and birds. The same analogy holds for temperate forests and also applies to backyard planning.

Different layers help to meet the needs of birds. Birds seldom spend all of their time in one layer. Chipping sparrows, for example, feed largely on the seeds of low-growing plants such as crabgrass and clover, but they nest in shrubs from three to ten feet off the ground and sing from the highest trees in their territory. Such observations suggest that multi-level habitats will provide edges in a vertical direction and will better meet the needs of a variety of birds.

This idea is helpful in many habitat improvement situations. If you have forest on your property or tall trees growing from a bare lawn

below, you can greatly improve the bird value of your woodland by planting mixed forest ground covers such as bunchberry or lowbush blueberries. Shrub and understory layers such as flowering dogwood or serviceberries will add more feeding and nesting layers to the woodland. Virginia creeper, wild grape, cat-brier and other vines should be encouraged wherever they become established. They add valuable food and nesting cover and help to connect the various layers.

Careful selection of different height plants also helps to create better habitats in a horizontal direction. For example, plant tall coniferous trees (e.g., spruce or pine) at the border of your property, shorter fruit-bearing trees (e.g., mountain-ash or flowering dogwood) in front of them, tall shrubs (e.g., elderberry, tatarian honeysuckle, or sargent crabapple as the next belt in the planting), followed by smaller shrubs (e.g., snowberry, coralberry or blackberry). Finally at the edge of the small shrubs, plant ground covers with bird-attracting value (e.g., creeping juniper, bearberry or crowberry).

Selecting Plants

Commonly used shrubs such as lilac, forsythia and azaleas have little value to birds. Instead, consider planting shrubs with both ornamental and bird-attracting value. Flowering dogwood,

Water, whether a pool, pond or birdbath, will attract a variety of birds to the backyard. Here a flock of robins bathe.
Photo by Hugh M. Halliday—The National Audubon Society (Photo Researchers, Inc.)

Flowering dogwood such as the Cornus florida *above provides color in the garden as well as cover and food for wild birds.*
Photo by Roche

honeysuckle, hollies and mountain-ash provide not only color, but cover and food for wild birds.

When selecting plantings for attracting wild birds, avoid exotics (plants native to other countries) in favor of native plants. Native plants have demonstrated ability to survive our climate and are unlikely to overrun other plants. Oriental bittersweet, kudzu, Japanese honeysuckle and multiflora rose are all vivid examples of "wonder plants" or exotics that became aggressive pests.

Editor's Note: A discussion of recommended North American ground covers, vines, shrubs and various-height trees for attracting birds is too vast a topic for this article. Let me refer the reader to this author's *Audubon Society Guide to Attracting Birds* (1985 Charles Scribner's Sons, New York).

Changes in Slope

Just as layering of vegetation is more attractive to birds, so too are changes in the slope of your property—especially where rock outcrops are exposed. Many ground-feeding birds such as wrens, towhees and white-throated sparrows are attracted to abrupt changes in slope. In natural habitats, these birds frequent stream banks, rock outcroppings, upturned tree roots and other unusual changes in slope.

If you have a new home and your yard is to be shaped by a bulldozer, protect irregularities in the contour of your property (such as natural outcrops of bedrock) by requesting the contractor to vary the slope of the yard where possible. Smaller scale changes in slope may be created by building a mound with a steep rock face or by creating rock gardens or stone walls. In northern climates, the steep surface of an artificial slope should face south so that the first spring thaw will reveal foraging places previously hidden by snow.

Hedges and different planting levels are a significant means of attracting a variety of birds to your property.
Photo by Roche

Providing Nesting Places

Properties with excellent food-production, cover and water may still not support their potential bird populations. There must also be adequate nest sites. Many perching birds—catbirds, thrashers and goldfinches—build their nests in tree or shrub crotches. Careful examination of the actual nest sites shows that most birds build where three or more branches emerge from about the same location on a main stem. This gives the nest maximum support. Pruning to create such nest sites may increase the chance of birds selecting your shrub(s) for their nests.

Dozens of North American birds, ranging in size from vultures to warblers nest in tree cavities. A dead branch or tree is a likely place for a natural tree cavity. Songbirds will use tall dead snags as singing posts while birds of prey sometimes use them to sight their next meal. With this in mind, it's important to preserve some dead tree snags on your property.

If you do not have conspicuous tree cavities, consider hanging nest boxes. The availability of suitable cavities is a common limiting factor; providing the right size nest box is one of the simplest things you can do to increase the number and variety of birds on your property.

Sacrifice Some Lawn for Mixed Ground Covers

A few birds, such as robins, grackles and flickers will feed in low-cropped lawns, but well-manicured yards are seldom visited by most birds. Where chemicals are used to control weeds or lawn insects, such yards may be a serious hazard to birds. A small patch of lawn has a useful place in a bird-attracting program as a focal place from which we can better see birds in more desirable habitats.

Many ground-feeding birds, such as towhees, thrashers and several native sparrows prefer feeding in leaf litter where they can scratch or poke for insects, earthworms and other invertebrates. A good place to create leaf-litter areas is under trees or shrubs where grasses have difficulty growing. Such areas can even be expanded by several feet in front of shrubs. Rake leaves into these areas each fall and let them decompose over the winter. By spring, the decomposed leaves will create ideal conditions for earthworms and other natural bird foods. These leaf-litter feeders may be easily maintained with an ordered look by edging them with flush flagstone borders that do not hamper mowing.

Further ground cover improvements can be achieved by planting borders and patches of low-growing perennial plants such as bearberry, crowberry, and creeping cotoneaster. The fruit produced by these perennial ground covers makes them more useful to birds than some of the more conventional ground covers such as pachysandra, periwinkle and Boston ivy.

Backyard Water Supplies

Open water throughout the year is an important feature of bird-attracting properties. This is especially important in arid regions or in northern habitats over winter. The simplest way to keep water from freezing in birdbaths and small pools is to install an electric water heater. These are available from stores that sell bird feed or from poultry supply houses.

Even a small birdbath positioned on a pedestal (the kind available for a few dollars at any garden shop) will do wonders for attracting birds. Success will be greatly improved by adding movement to the water. A simple way to accomplish this is to hang a bucket with a hole in the bottom over the birdbath. This slow water drip is a simple, but proven way to lure birds to water. The variety of birds attracted by this simple technique is amazing—especially during migration when warblers and vireos join the more usual visitors.

Where space permits, an in-ground bird pool can be a delightful addition to your property. This can be a beautiful addition to a rock garden, especially if creatively landscaped with ferns and other low ground covers. The simplest way to build such a pool is to excavate a hole and line it with heavy black plastic. The contour of the slope is a key consideration; it should be no more than three inches deep and should slope gently on the sides.

A more permanent and natural-looking pool can be created using concrete mix. First excavate the site, digging about nine inches deep (six inches if you live in a non-freezing latitude), taking care to grade the sides at a gentle slope.

If you live in an area where soils freeze in the winter, fill the hole with several inches of sand to reduce the risk of frost heaving it in the winter. To give added strength to the concrete, cut a piece of welded wire (one by two-inch mesh) to fit the hole, pressing it down over the sand. Pour three inches of concrete mix over the wire so that it is buried inside the concrete.

Dust Bathing

Many birds bathe in both water and dust. House sparrows, quail, hawks and even tiny kinglets "splash" about in the dust, just as they would in water. The reasons for dusting are not clear, but it's likely a means of displacing irritating parasites such as feather lice. It may also serve to remove excess oil and moisture that would otherwise cause feather matting. Dusting areas are a means for luring birds into view. If you build a dusting bath, position it in a conspicuous place, far from cover that might hide predatory cats. Dusting birds seem especially oblivious to approaching predators.

Dusting baths may be as small as a foot square, but larger baths can accommodate more birds simultaneously. To create a dust bath, excavate a six-inch-deep depression and line the edge with bricks or rocks. Then fill the depression with a dust mix consisting of one-third each of sand, loam and sifted ash.

Food Patches

An easy way to produce more bird food and reduce the amount of close-cropped lawn in your yard, is to simply let some grain go to seed. Often wildflowers with bird-attracting value, such as thistle, black-eyed susan and clover will soon dominate such patches.

Studies of the stomach contents of wild birds consistently point to the importance of weed seeds as food. To create a natural food patch, all you need do is till the soil. It is likely that some of the most important wild bird foods will grow without even planting. The seeds of ragweed, amaranth, lambsquarters, sheep sorrel, bristle grass and panic grass are widely distributed in most soils—ready to germinate upon soil disturbance.

Depending on space, a wild food patch can be a 100 to 2,000 square foot patch of tilled soil. If space permits, till three strips in rotation over successive years. Long, narrow patches are better than square plots, since they offer more edge. Mown walkways between the strips will give your natural food plots an orderly appearance.

Cultivated crops can provide a concentrated food supply over a short period. Cultivated food patches are easily grown by broadcasting a bag of mixed seed over freshly tilled soil. A 15 pound bag of mixed seed is enough to grow a half-acre patch of millet, milo and sunflower.

Like the grain dispensed from bird feeders, cultivated food patches are a short-term solution to bird food needs. Their use should be supplementary to other natural food supplies such as meadows, thickets and forests with their abundant bird-attracting vegetation.

Garden Flowers for the Birds

Just as some trees and shrubs have both ornamental and bird-attracting value, the same applies to garden flowers. When selecting flowers for your garden, keep birds in mind and choose some of their favorites. Most of the garden flowers recommended for birds are members of the sunflower family. Sunflowers (of all sizes) are especially attractive to goldfinches, sparrows and other members of the finch family.

Most of the flowers in the following lists will grow in moist, summer gardens throughout North America. With few exceptions, they require open, sunlit growing space. Garden flowers should be fertilized with one to two pounds of general purpose fertilizer per 100 square feet. Water, but do not soak and be sure to leave the flower heads on so that the birds can consume the ripened seeds in the fall and winter.

Selected Garden Flowers For Attracting Wild Birds

For Sunny Sites

Aster *(Aster spp.)*
Bachelor's buttons *(Centaurea americana)*
Blessed thistle *(Cnicus benedictus)*
Calendula *(Calendula officinalis)*
California poppy *(Eschscholzia californica)*
Campanula *(Campanula spp.)*
China aster *(Callistephus chinensis)*
Chrysanthemum *(Chrysanthemum spp.)*
Coneflowers *(Rudbeckia spp.)*

Cornflowers *(Centaurea spp.)*
Cosmos *(Cosmos spp.)*
Dusty miller *(Centaurea cineraria)*
Love-lies-bleeding *(Amaranthus caudatus)*
Marigolds *(Tagetes spp.)*
Phlox *(Phlox spp.* especially *P. drummondii)*
Prince's feather *(Celosia cristata)*
Silene *(Silene spp.)*
Sunflower *(Helianthus annuus)*
Sweet scabiosa *(Scabiosa atropurpurea)*
Verbena *(Verbena hybrida)*
Zinnia *(Zinnia elegans)*

For Sites with Light Shade

Basket flower *(Centaurea americana)*
Coreopsis *(Coreopsis spp.)*
Dayflowers *Commelina spp.)*
Sweet sultan *(Centaurea moschata)*

Landscaping for Hummingbirds

In the western United States at least 14 hummingbird species regularly visit gardens with hummingbird-attracting plants. Some western hummers, such as Anna's hummingbird, frequent backyards throughout the year. In the eastern United States and southeastern Canada, only the ruby-throated hummingbird occurs, but it is often very responsive to sympathetic gardeners. A dozen or more may swarm over a flowering tree such as mimosa or horse-chestnut.

Although hummingbirds are primarily nectar-eaters and obtain their liquid meals deep within flowers, they also eat large quantities of insects and spiders which they snatch from flowers. Planting flowers to attract hummingbirds provides the hummers with a two-course meal of nectar and insects.

You can attract hummingbirds to your garden by planting trees, shrubs or garden flowers with tubular shaped blooms. Hummingbirds prefer orange or red flowers, but they will also visit pink, purple, blue and even some white flowers. An important goal of any hummingbird garden should be to plant the flowers in large, conspicuous clumps and to select varieties that bloom from spring through late summer.

Based on the idea of layered vegetation, you can attract hummingbirds to your garden by building a multi-level display of attractive plants. On the south-facing side of your home or outbuilding, establish a tall, climbing vine such as honeysuckle, trumpet-creeper, scarlet runner

A natural pond not only adds water for birds, but interest and increased habitats for herons, ducks and geese. Pond-edge plantings can increase the diversity of habitats.

bean, or morning glory. Surround the vine with shrubs such as bush fuchsia or weigela or plant tall annuals such as zinnia and phlox. Shorter garden flowers; e.g. columbine or beebalm, are excellent choices for a border.

Another successful design for a hummingbird garden is to centrally plant a tree (horse-chestnut, red buckeye or mimosa) and to hang baskets of fuchsia from the branches. Plant several varieties of impatiens in the shade under the tree.

Plants for Attracting Hummingbirds

Northern Gardens

American Columbine *(Aquilegia canadensis)*
Beebalm *(Monarda didyma)*
Bugleweed *(Ajuga reptans)*
Butterfly milkweed *(Asclepias tuberosa)*
Cardinal flower *(Lobelia cardinalis)*
Coralberry *(Symphoricarpos orbiculatus)*

Fuchsias *(Fuchsia spp.)*; vines and shrubs
Hibiscus *(Hibiscus spp.* especially *H. syriacus)*
Hollyhocks *(Althea spp.)*
Horse-chestnut *(Aesculus hippocastanum)*
Jewelweeds *(Impatiens capensis* and *I. pallida)*
Larkspur *(Delphinium spp.)*
Madrone *(Arbutus menziesii)*
Ohio buckeye *(Aesculus glabra)*
Evening primrose *(Oenothera spp.)*
Siberian pea tree *(Caragana arborescens)*
Tiger lily *(Lilium tigrinum)*
Trumpet honeysuckle *(Lonicera sempervirens)*
Trumpet vine *(Campsis radicans)*
Zinnia *(Zinnia elegans)*

Southern Gardens
(most from northern list are also appropriate)

Citrus tree *(Citrus spp.)*; low trees
Coral bean *(Erythrina spp.)*
Fire pink *(Silene virginiana)*
Lemon bottlebrush *(Callistemon lanceolatus)*
Mimosa tree *(Albizia julibrissin)*
Red buckeye *(Aesculus pavia)*
Scarlet runner bean *(Phaseolus coccineus)*
Weigela *(Weigela spp.)* 🐦

Bright Berries for the Garden, Food for the Birds

Helen Van Pelt Wilson

S mall trees and shrubs that hold their fruits through the coldest months offer fine color accents for the winter garden, and also food for the birds whose bright plumage sparkles in the cold air. Birds like the gray berries of the bayberry, as well as the darker blue fruits of red cedar, privet, and hackberry. However, these do not provide color for the garden and so may have to be omitted, except on very large properties, in favor of the brightest plants. Sumac, though also red-berried and favored by many birds, is too coarse a plant except for extensive wild areas.

The choice of really handsome red-berried material for winter seems infinite. Some of it, like the dogwood, is fairly familiar. Much of it, especially among varieties of hawthorn, euonymus, holly, and viburnum, is less well known. In the charts at the end of this article are plants that make an undoubtedly stunning collection, since all have been chosen for brilliance, hardiness, and long-season color effect. Some, like the barberries, actually retain their berries until the next year's blosssoms insist that they give way.

Aside from the sheer beauty of their fruit and the rich tones of early winter foliage, these are the trees and shrubs that attract the garden birds which devour the juicy fruits earlier in summer

Helen Van Pelt Wilson has written more than a dozen books on such subjects as perennials, geraniums, flower arranging and home gardening. She is an internationally known editor and speaker.

Snowberry (Symphoricarpos albus) *bears white berries into winter. A favorite shrub of 25 species of birds.*

Photo by Roche.

Mountain ash (Sorbus aucuparia) *is an outstanding fruiting ornamental enjoyed by up to 15 species of birds. It bears red-to-orange berries for a long season—August to February.*

and fall, and the dried, somewhat bitter ones last. In mild winters the birds leave many of these for the gardener also to enjoy, but in seasons of snow and stress, when normal food supplies are cut down to about two percent, they will feast even upon the enduring fruit of the firethorn.

In winter, in addition to berries, birds often feed on the "cones" of alders, birches, and sweet gums. When the wind strikes these, the seeds are blown out onto the ground to the delight of goldfinches and others. I like to see them worrying the tiny cones of the ancient hemlocks outside my windows. Woodpeckers, blue jays, and nuthatches come to my feeders, but they also eat the acorns of the pin oak. If you have a tall Colorado or Norway spruce, or a white or Scotch pine on your place, you will very likely see the birds eating their seeds and also welcoming the shelter of the evergreen branches.

Trees with Berries

It is often difficult to label some plants *trees* and others *shrubs*. Many kinds can be treated either way. It all depends on pruning. The simplest distinction is that a woody plant grown with one trunk is a tree, while a shrub has several or many main stems. So, considering their usual manner of growth, I select among berried trees the Washington thorn, dogwood, American holly, another holly, *Ilex decidua* (the possum haw), and the glorious mountain ash.

In any garden of less than an acre, where trees are wanted principally for shade, one of these might be given room for its bright fruit, and then, perhaps, one or more of the shrubby types can be added. Most of these berried plants are dominant growers, strong, lusty, and wanting room; they are particularly handsome when allowed a free range for their talents. Hence satisfaction is greater when they are used as prominent specimens and allowed to develop a natural, unpruned shape. You will notice that the berried crops are usually heavier in alternate years.

The Washington thorn, *Crataegus phaenopyrum (cordata)*, is an amazingly beautiful tree, especially when seen under a blue October sky, with its scarlet foliage a background for a tremendous abundance of large, shiny red corymbs of fruit. These persist colorfully even into March, being among the last to attract the birds, which prefer softer and juicier fruit. Native from Virginia to Alabama and Missouri, the Washington thorn is hardy in New York and Boston, too, where it eventually reaches a dignified 25 to 30 feet. If there is room for it, this Washington thorn may be grandly planted in a driveway or boundary row.

The flowering dogwood, *Cornus florida,* is the special treasure of Philadelphia and Valley Forge, where the plantings are unusually massive and lovely. In one of my own early gardens, I had a treasured pair of shapely specimens planted beside a brick entrance walk. At no season were they anything but commandingly beautiful. In October the foliage turned a gorgeous crimson and the shining berries studded the branches for weeks into early winter (the number of weeks depending on the appetites of the birds—and also on the appeal of the fruit to squirrels, who can clean up a crop in a few days). More than 85 kinds of birds, the records show, look on the glistening red dogwood berries as item number one on their favorite menus. I gladly shared my crop with robins, cardinals, and others, since the fruiting season is but one of the attractions of the dogwood. Native from

Massachusetts to Florida, and West to Ontario and Texas, this dogwood seems to have everything.

The American holly, *Ilex opaca,* is another general favorite, although it is planted less often than it might be because of a misapprehension concerning its manner of fruiting. Since this holly is dioecious (that is, with male and female flowers on separate specimens), two specimens must be included in a planting to ensure berries. The female tree may be prominently planted and the male—lacking conspicuous fruits, and smaller perhaps, but still an attractive evergreen—may be inconspicuously placed in the shrubbery border.

From the standpoint of berries, American holly is particularly desirable, because its glory is a winter matter. An evergreen, it dots itself with red in late November and at Christmas time becomes the very symbol of the season. Move it any time from fall to spring when the ground is not frozen, but preferably in early fall when the young wood has almost ripened, or in the spring before growth starts. The ideal location for holly is a partially shaded spot with protection from west wind. The soil must be well drained, acid, and preferably sandy. A three-inch mulch of peat moss is excellent, especially during the first year. Under such conditions the American holly will grow to 40 feet and endure with equanimity the rigors of even hard winters.

Ilex decidua is a gem of a small tree growing some 20 feet high. As the name indicates, it is not evergreen. Southern nurseries usually carry it, but in the North it is hard to find because it is considered tender—though this is not the case, since this holly has survived 17 degrees below zero in Philadelphia. Native from Virginia to Florida and west to Texas, *I. decidua,* thickly covered with large red fruits, suggests a cherry tree bearing its bright burden somewhat late in the season. Such is its form, although the bark is pale gray. It is definitely among the very finest of berried plants, beautiful enough to search for diligently. Self-pollinating, this holly is little trouble to grow and produces large, attractive fruit. Coming from swampy areas, it needs plenty of water.

The Bright Shrubs

Among the berried shrubs, there is another deciduous holly to consider, *Ilex verticillata,* the common winterberry or black alder. Native to eastern North America, from Nova Scotia to western Ontario and Missouri, it grows some nine feet high and spreads to 15 feet, a superb plant at the height of its autumn grandeur. Like many hollies, it is dioecious, requiring both male and female plants for pollination. It is among our most adaptable natives, growing equally well in swampy or dry land, in sun or

Rosa rugosa 'Blanc Double de Coubert' pictured below is a thick growing plant which provides birds with good cover and winter protection. It is also a good candidate for seashore conditions.
Photo by Roche

shade. Its shade tolerance is, of course, a valuable asset, since most of the berry-bearers demand the sun. The verticillata fruit is coral-red and thickly distributed along the stem. In October the yellow-green of the foliage turns bronze and really glimmers in the sun. In the Pennsylvania mountains it has earned the name fire bush. Birds do not immediately strip it as they may the dogwood, but by early winter the fire (fruit) is likely to be gone.

An attractive upright shrub for the edge of a woodland or the forefront of a mixed shrub border, the native red chokeberry, *Aronia*

arbutifolia, offers a big crop of red berries that lasts well into winter, and if the planting is in the sun, the autumn foliage will turn a fine red to set off the crop of fruit.

Juniperus virginiana *of dense, green foliage provides 39 species of birds with a good wintertime supply of food and cover.*

The barberry family is famous for at least one variety, *Berberis thunbergii* or Japanese barberry. In trimmed hedges it will ever be pathetic to me, but planted either as a hedge or as a specimen where space is not limited and the pruning shears are withheld, it becomes something grand, with sparkling berries like ladies' earrings hanging in gay abundance from each blazing, foliaged branch. And these cling on to adorn the bare branches all winter long. Less familiar, and highly recommended, is the Korean barberry, *B. koreana,* handsome in foliage, in flower, and particularly in fruit, which also hangs in glowing clusters. The dense growth creates an impenetrable barrier.

Where a low plant is desirable, there is the rockspray, *Cotoneaster horizontalis,* one of two particularly handsome members of the cotoneaster group. It has flat, spraying branches, perfect for foaming over a low wall or hanging above a slope. It may even serve as a ground cover. Semievergreen in the North, evergreen and fruiting heavily in the South, this shrub endures hot, dry, sunny situations and puts on

a beautiful September and October show by studding its branches thickly with a display of scarlet berries and orange-to-red foliage.

The firethorn, *Pyracantha coccinea,* especially the 'Lalandei' variety, is one of the most magnificent of the fruiting shrubs. It looks to me like an autumn-leaf bonfire that has got a little out of hand and is burning madly on just to please itself. The heavily clustered fruit is orange with all the brilliance of flame, and it may remain into late January. The ultimate height of the shrub is six feet and the spread is to 10 feet; grown as a vine it may reach eight feet in height. A well-grown specimen in the fruiting season is indeed a grand sight, but whether the birds will strip it early of its ornaments is a question. The claim is made for a September-to-March display in some areas that seventeen species of birds enjoy.

A shrub rose, *R. rugosa,* is a tall, "rough," spreading plant to grow outside the garden proper. I have enjoyed this plant set along the far side of a post-and-rail fence. The purple-red blooms of the rugosas open over a long period. The "hips," as the orange-red fruits are called, delight the birds. The dense growth of this species of rose offers winter protection as well as food and nesting sites in spring. This shrub rose

Editor's Note: Also see pg. 17 and pgs. 48-49 for charts on those plants that are particular favorites of hummingbirds.

grows well at the seashore. Today there are many hybrids and named varieties, with summer-blooming flowers in various tints of pink, crimson, yellow, and white; the habit of shrubby, thorny, year-round growth is invaluable.

The Japanese skimmia *(S. japonica)* has proved far hardier for me in Zone 6, where the temperature only occasionally falls below zero, than is generally claimed. Broader than it is high, this four-foot shrub produces fragrant spring flowers followed by clusters of scarlet berries that do not appeal to the birds until most other supplies are exhausted late in winter. Both male and female plants are required for fruiting, the male grown in an inconspicuous spot. I grew skimmias successfully in a somewhat shaded, northeastern location inside a stone wall that protected them from wind. If the temperature in your garden does not go below zero, the spectacular berried skimmia will be fairly safe and a handsome addition to your winter garden. You might plant the female shrubs for bright effect in front of the tall rhododendrons or azaleas that also require a somewhat acid soil and a good mulch. Another species, of recent introduction, *S. reevesiana,* grows to somewhat less height, is hardy to Zone 7, and bears perfect flowers, hence will be fertilized and produce fruits. The leaves are dull green but the berries are prolific in the fall and, in sheltered places, last even into January.

One shrub with white fruits, the snowberry, *Symphoricarpos albus,* is a treasure to lighten a shaded area. It is low-growing and excellent for the front of the shrub border where this passes out of the sun; the snowberry shows up well in early winter when the leaves have fallen and the white berries are silhouetted against the dark green of hemlocks or against a group of taller broad-leaved shrubs like mountain laurel or Japanese andromeda. I am glad to see that nurserymen are offering snowberries again.

Although the viburnum genus is chiefly famous because it contains the common snowball, it includes far more distinguished members. The high-bush cranberry, *Viburnum trilobum* or *americanum,* has long pleased both me and the birds. Extremely hardy even to Zone 2, this spreading native shrub offers clusters of bright red fruits all through winter. So, too, does the European cranberry, *V. opulus,* with vivid red, bitter berries that become transparent and also stay through winter.

Fruiting Vines

Four handsome vines produce winter-long berries but all four are for special situations. I grow the evergreen (really semievergreen) bittersweet, *Euonymus fortunei,* against the divider on the south side, also along the picket fence. This small-leaved vine grows to six feet fairly quickly here, but must reach greater maturity before it produces berries for a late-winter meal for the birds. It is one of the most attractive of the evergreen vines. (In the same genus, *E. patens* is not a vine but a grand hedge plant and fruits only in the South; *E. sachalinensis* is a great spreading semievergreen shrub with bright red fuchsialike flowers, effective where there is space for it.)

The Virginia creeper or woodbine, *Parthenocissus quinquefolia,* and Boston ivy, *P. tricuspidata,* are for house walls or old stone fences. Both have dark blue berries that have the advantage of hanging on through winter and appealing to many birds, but neither has the garden appeal of a red-berried shrub.

For the winter garden, trees and shrubs with bright berries are a fine sight, particularly in association with evergreens—and a nice light fall of snow. Plant your berry-bearers in good view of the house, where you can watch the birds enjoying the fruits. In time, Virginia creeper and Boston ivy will completely enframe the windows of a brick house, and thrushes, robins, finches and sparrows can often be plainly seen resting or pausing on the windowsill.

You can see in the chart that follows what wealth of attractive berried material you can select to decorate your yard or garden. You may have room for only one tree and, perhaps, three or four of these shrubs, for most of them require considerable space, but these are all plants that add to the beauty of the winter landscape as they attract the birds that in winter are colorful substitutes for the flowers of summer.

Trees, Shrubs, and Vines with Winter Berries

The length of time these plants hold their berries varies with their location, the weather, and the onslaught of the birds in some seasons. A flock may arrive to strip a plant one year and leave the berries on the same plant until spring another year. In the cross-references the most familiar common name is used, as Privet instead of Regel Privet. 🦋

NAME	ZONE*	HEIGHT IN FEET	BERRIES FOR BIRDS	COMMENTS
Aronia arbutifolia Red Chokeberry	4-9	9	Small, effective white flowers in spring; abundant fall crop of red berries lasting well into winter; spectacular red autumn foliage.	For moist or dry soil in light to deep shade; large, native shrub of irregular form.
Barberry, see *Berberis* Bayberry, see *Myrica*				
Berberis koreana Korean Barberry	4-9	4	Yellow flowers in mid-May; red autumn foliage, with pendent clusters of brilliant orange-red fruits that color in fall and hang on well into winter.	Thorny twigs; deciduous shrub with spreading, arching growth. A good substitute for *B. vulgaris,* which carries wheat rust.
B. thunbergii Japanese Barberry	4-9	4-5	Small white flowers in spring; berries strung along stems last through winter longer than those of any other shrub; scarlet autumn foliage.	Endures deep shade, dry soil; makes a prickly barrier or bank plant for sun or shade. Dependable even in worst situations. Variety 'Minor' is 12″ to 18″ with dense growth; good for low, red hedge.
Black Alder, see *Ilex* Boston Ivy, see *Parthenocissus* Cedar, see *Juniperus*				
Celtis occidentalis Hackberry	3-7	80	High, branching tree with seedy blue berries favored by at least 35 bird species.	Berries persist through fall, winter, and spring. Not for small properties.
Cornus florida Flowering Dogwood	4-9	25	Shiny red berries sought by 85 species through fall and early winter. Sometimes squirrels get there first. Crimson autumn foliage.	Handsome small tree with horizontal branches for open lawn or in the shade of other trees where there is shifting sunlight. Prune flat or let droop gracefully toward the ground. Needs deep watering in drought.
C. kousa Japanese Dogwood	5-8	20	Smaller dogwood with fleshy pink-red fruits resembling strawberries; nice to have both dogwoods.	Bushy growth, very shade-tolerant; blooms 3 weeks after *C. florida.*
Cotoneaster horizontalis Rockspray	4-9	3	June flowers followed by red fruits; more prolific in warm areas; semievergreen.	Horizontal branching makes this valuable for foaming over walls, training as an espalier, or use as ground cover.

NAME	ZONE*	HEIGHT IN FEET	BERRIES FOR BIRDS	COMMENTS
Crabapple, see *Malus*				
Cranberry Bush, see *Viburnum*				
Crataegus phaenopyrum (cordata) Washington Thorn	4-8	25	Rounded thorny native tree with red berries to please 33 species in winter if robins and cedar waxwings do not strip tree first; scarlet autumn foliage.	One of the last hawthorns to bloom; more spectacular in winter fruit than in spring flower. Fruit so heavy it looks like a second blooming. Avoid proximity to junipers because of rust. Deep rooting; tolerates shade. Good city tree.
Dogwood, see *Cornus*				

Malus 'Red Jade' is a weeping crabapple tree
that is often covered with small brightly-colored
fruits that attract many birds. This crabapple
was developed by BBG.

NAME	ZONE*	HEIGHT IN FEET	BERRIES FOR BIRDS	COMMENTS
Euonymus fortunei 'Vegeta' Evergreen Bittersweet	5-9	20	Bright orange fruits often in good condition from winter into spring; birds finally eat them.	Really semievergreen; can be trained as vine or left unpruned as a shrub that piles up its horizontal branches. Plant all in semi-shade to avoid scale.
E. kiautschovica (patens) Spreading Euonymus	6-9	7	Green-white flowers; early Sept. in South; late pinkish or red fruits where growing season long enough.	Handsome spreading evergreen for North but without fruits there. Good hedge plant.
E. sachalinensis (planipes)	5-8	12	Bright crimson fall leaves; large, pendent bright red fruits like fuchsia flowers hang in profusion on into winter.	From northeast Asia and Japan, a semievergreen shrub spreading to 12'. Interesting for unusual and abundant fruits.

Evergreen Bittersweet, see *Euonymus*
Firethorn, see *Pyracantha*
Hackberry, see *Celtis*
Holly, see *Ilex*

NAME	ZONE*	HEIGHT IN FEET	BERRIES FOR BIRDS	COMMENTS
Ilex decidua Possum Haw	5-8	20	Bright orange-red berries held well into winter, often longer.	Southeastern native deciduous tree with lustrous foliage. Self-pollinating, needs plenty of water.
I. opaca American Holly	5-9	40	Favorite with 45 species for red berries well into Feb. and dense protective foliage.	Spectacular native evergreen tree, bushy or pyramidal. Male tree is essential for pollination but can be small and unimportantly placed. Hollies endure quite damp situations and prefer partial shade.
I. verticillata Winterberry or Black Alder	3-9	9	Large deciduous holly. Bright red berries for early winter for 22 species.	A shrub with a 15' spread. Best in acid soil. Also a dwarf variety to 3' tall with very large berries.

Japanese Dogwood, see *Cornus*

NAME	ZONE*	HEIGHT IN FEET	BERRIES FOR BIRDS	COMMENTS
Juniperus virginiana 'Canaertii' Red Cedar	2-9	10	Abundance of bluish berries and dense, dark green foliage supply both food and winter cover for 39 species throughout the winter.	Pyramidal, slow-growing form of native red cedar; excellent specimen for full sun, drought-tolerant. Makes a good evergreen hedge, but not as effective in winter garden as redberried shrubs, except as back-line for small gardens.

NAME	ZONE*	HEIGHT IN FEET	BERRIES FOR BIRDS	COMMENTS
Ligustrum obtusifolium regelianum Regel Privet	3-8	4-5	Most graceful of privets; birds delight in the blue-black berries and winter protection of twiggy horizontal branches.	Small glossy leaves; plants withstand city conditions; hardy in light, not deep, shade.
Malus 'Dorothea' Crabapple	4-8	25	Semidouble pink flowers in May; yellow fruits from fall to early winter.	One of very few double-flower crabapples to produce ornamental fruit; attractive tree for small property.
Mountain Ash, see *Sorbus*				
Myrica pensylvanica Bayberry	2-8	6	Abundance of waxy, gray berries favored by at least 73 species.	Rangy, semievergreen shrub, aromatic foliage; for light or deep shade; tolerates poor soil, some dampness, good for seacoast.
Parthenocissus quinquefolia Virginia Creeper or Woodbine	3-8	50	Rambling native vine with fine fall color and a wealth of blue-black berries that hang on to Feb. for 37 species.	Vines usually grown on house walls but also makes pleasing covering for New England stone fences; has 5 large leaflets.
P. tricuspidata Boston Ivy	4-8	50	Glowing scarlet autumn foliage; dark blue fruit hardly visible until leaves fall, then decorative until late winter.	Boston ivy has 3 leaflets (same as poison ivy); not to grow against wood. Will reach the top of a 3-story house. Birds may nest in the woody growth.
Possum Haw, see *Ilex*				
Privet, see *Ligustrum*				
Pyracantha coccinea Firethorn	5-8	6-8	Inconspicuous but charming white spring flowers; gorgeous orange-red berries all winter unless stripped early; enjoyed by 17 species.	Grown as a broad shrub or tall trellised vine; needs full sun or early morning sun, protected location; almost evergreen. 'Lalandei' choice variety.
Red Chokeberry, see *Aronia*				
Rhus typhina Staghorn Sumac	3-8	15	Heads of dark red berries delight some 93 species and last Sept. –May.	Not for limited areas; coarse but spectacular for a grove. Stiff not graceful growth.
Rockspray, see *Cotoneaster*				

NAME	ZONE*	HEIGHT IN FEET	BERRIES FOR BIRDS	COMMENTS
Rosa rugosa Rugosa Rose	3-8	5-8	Dense, spreading with a wealth of orange-red fruit, called "hips," that birds flock to; thick growth makes fine winter protection and nesting sites. Well suited to seashore conditions.	Long season; purple-red blooms and cultivars with white, pink, and yellow flowers. 'Frau Dagmar Hartopp,' a smaller white-flowering plant, also produces rose hips that please the birds.
Rose, see *Rosa* Rowan, see *Sorbus*				
Skimmia japonica Japanese Skimmia	7-8	4	Fragrant white flowers in spring; bright red berries, bitter-tasting, left by birds till last.	Handsome evergreen; male pollinator necessary for fruiting. Hardy for me in Zone 6, grown next to a protecting stone wall.
Snowberry, see *Symphoricarpos*				
Sorbus aucuparia European Mountain Ash or Rowan	2-7	45	Flat white flower clusters in May–June; glowing bright-red-to-orange berries Aug. – Feb.; 15 species enjoy them.	Handsome tree for moist to dry soil in sun. One of the most outstanding of fruiting ornamentals.
Sumac, see *Rhus*				
Symphoricarpos albus laevigatus Snowberry	3-9	2-5	White-berried shrub effective in front of evergreens or other tall plants; large fruits last into winter and are favored by 25 species.	Makes a good thicket in deep shade; may bend to ground when weighted by fruit; thrives in dry soil. 'Mother of Pearl' hybrid with pink berries.
Viburnum opulus European Cranberry Bush	3-7	12	Dense growth; orange-to-red autumn leaves; vivid red, bitter berries that become transparent as they stay on through winter.	Effective massed for color of white May flower and red fruits; stands dryness and heat. 'Compactum' to 5'; 'Xanthocarpum' with yellow fruits.
V. trilobum (americanum) American Cranberry Bush or High-Bush Cranberry	2-5	10	Spreading native shrub with clusters of glossy scarlet berries that hang on through winter; food for 34 species.	More cold-tolerant than most viburnums. Effective winter shrub especially in snow. Oval berries first yellow on one side, red on the other, then all red.

Virginia Creeper, see
Parthenocissus
Washington Thorn, see
Crataegus
Winterberry, see *Ilex*
Woodbine, see *Parthenocissus*

* *Ed. note: The zones apply to the USDA climate zone map.*

Firethorn (Pyracantha coccinea) *is a favorite food for 17 species of birds.*

Photo by Roche

Attracting Cavity-Nesting Birds To Gardens And Woodlots

Robert A. Askins

Many natural features that attract birds are easy to work into a garden. Water, dense shrub cover, and berry-producing plants can be used in a number of different landscape designs. Few such designs can easily accommodate dead and dying trees, however, and these are crucially important to a large number of bird species. Snags and dead branches provide sites for nesting, roosting and feeding. In Canada and the United States 85 species of birds nest in cavities in dead trees or branches,[1] and approximately one-fourth of the forest-dwelling mammals and birds in the Northeast depend upon dead trees for den or nest sites.[2] A manicured garden or a "well-managed" woodlot will lack these species unless there is a wilder area with dead trees nearby.

Use of Dead Trees by Birds

Birds that nest in cavities can be divided into two groups: primary excavators, birds that dig out cavities in wood, and secondary users, which use abandoned holes of primary excavators or cavities resulting from decay. Woodpeckers are the most important primary excavators because they can dig cavities in hard, dead wood or even in living branches which have a soft, decayed heartwood. These cavities are much more suitable as nest sites than most natural cavities because they have a small entrance hole sur-

Dr. Robert A. Askins is Associate Professor of Zoology at Connecticut College. He is the author of numerous papers on fluctuations in breeding bird populations caused by isolation of habitats.

At left is pictured a pileated woodpecker. These birds prefer to nest in dense forests but are adapting to human encroachment and seem to tolerate disturbed habitats. Their main food is carpenter ants in rotting trees and stumps.

rounded by sound wood that is not easily penetrated by raccoons and other predators. In contrast, chickadees, which are also primary excavators, dig nest holes in soft, rotten wood. Eastern deciduous forests typically have four to six species of woodpeckers that make cavities of different sizes. Many species of secondary users, such as American kestrels, screech owls, tufted titmice, tree swallows, house wrens and eastern bluebirds, commonly nest in cavities made by woodpeckers. Secondary users sometimes take over recently completed woodpecker cavities, forcing the woodpeckers to build another cavity.[3] Starlings are especially adept at doing this. Secondary users can benefit from the building efforts of woodpeckers even when they do not take over their nests because each pair of woodpeckers builds a new cavity every year, probably to escape the nest parasites that infest old nests. A dense population of woodpeckers will therefore provide a continual supply of safe, abandoned nest holes that will support a diversity of other birds. Woodpeckers generally cannot build in living wood, however, so gardens and woodlots where snags are removed and unhealthy branches are pruned will not support nesting woodpeckers.

Secondary users are not completely dependent upon woodpeckers. They can also use natural cavities resulting from decay. White-breasted nuthatches prefer to nest in such tree hollows and brown creepers typically nest under loose bark on dead trees. These sites are scarce when dead trees and branches are systematically removed; in Europe it has been shown that hole-nesting species are much more abundant in unmanaged forests than in highly managed forests.[4]

Many species of birds depend upon cavities

31

not only during the breeding season, but also during the winter. These cavities provide a safe refuge from predators and protection from wind, precipitation and cold. Chickadees, nuthatches, creepers, bluebirds, wrens and woodpeckers all spend winter nights inside cavities. The temperature inside a cavity can be substantially higher than the outside temperature.[5] Birds spend more time in the winter inside their cavities than outside (winter nights are longer than winter days), so the extra insulation provided by the wood around a roost cavity is important for survival. Each woodpecker makes a cavity for roosting, and individuals sometimes construct two or more of them. Hence roost hole digging is another way in which woodpeckers increase the number of cavities available to other animals.

Woodpeckers sleep alone in their custom-built roost cavities, but many other species use old woodpecker holes or natural cavities more effectively by roosting in groups. When large numbers of individuals of the same species cluster together, the cavity provides both insulation and a source of warmth. Communal roosting has been reported in nuthatches, chickadees,

House wrens will nest in boxes when provided. They are very social birds and seem to enjoy nesting in suburban communities. Their bubbling song is sufficient reward for providing the nesting site.

The Birds, Bees and Butterflies

Female cardinal perches on berry and snow laden branches of black alder (Ilex verticillata).
Photo by Thase Daniel— (Bruce Coleman, Inc.)

Bee gathers nectar from the flowers of goldenrod (Solidago sp.)
Photo by Paul Frese

Below *Borders backed by shrubs and trees provide edges and diverse habitats for many species of wildlife. In the foreground* Aster x frickartii *is intermixed with Pinocchio rose.*
Photo by Paul Frese

Below right *Black-capped chickadee perches on the top of a sunflower picking out seeds.*

Photo by Gregory K. Scott—The National Audubon Society (Photo Researchers, Inc.)

Top right *An American painted lady butterfly matches and contrasts with the zinnia on which it has alighted.*
Photo by David Overcash—(Bruce Coleman, Inc.)

Left *An Anna's hummingbird visits the brightly colored flower of double-flowered hibiscus seeking nectar.*
Photo by Bob and Clara Calhoun—(Bruce Coleman, Inc.)

Top *A male evening grosbeak feeds on crabapples. During the winter months, these birds often travel in flocks.*
Photo by Gregory K. Scott—The National Audubon Society (Photo Researchers, Inc.)

Middle *The brilliant orange flowers of butterfly weed* (Asclepias tuberosa) *attract many species of butterflies.*
Photo by Paul Frese

Bottom *Feeders provide birds with food in the winter months when food is often scarce. Here a blue jay visits a snow-covered feeder.*
Photo by Harry Hartman—(Bruce Coleman, Inc.)

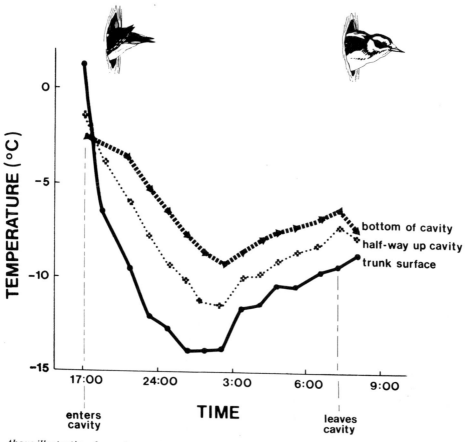

TEMPERATURE (°C)

bottom of cavity
half-way up cavity
trunk surface

17:00 24:00 3:00 6:00 9:00

TIME

enters
cavity

leaves
cavity

Above illustration shows changes in temperature in the roost cavity of a hairy woodpecker during a February night in Minnesota. Temperature probes were inserted through small holes drilled to the bottom of the cavity and half-way up the interior. The maximum difference in temperature between the bottom of the cavity and outside was 7° C (12° F).

Originally published in *The Loon,* Bell Museum of Natural History, 1981.

creepers, winter wrens, and eastern bluebirds[5]

Removal of dead and dying wood not only eliminates nesting and roosting sites, but also destroys a substantial food source for birds. Dead trees and branches have a rich supply of bark insects and wood-boring grubs that are important to many of the species that over-winter in the temperate zone. Creepers, nuthatches and chickadees subsist on insects and spiders extracted from crevices and cracks in the bark. Woodpeckers dig below the surface of the bark to extract grubs that bore through dead and decaying wood. My own research on woodpeckers in Minnesota and Maryland shows that three species (downy, hairy, and pileated woodpeckers) spend more than 50 per-

cent of their feeding time on dead trees and branches. Thus removal of dead wood is a triple blow for many forest birds; they are deprived of nest sites, winter shelter and an important source of food.

Substitutes for Dead Trees

Because secondary cavity users, such as wood ducks, tree swallows, tufted titmice, house wrens and bluebirds, will readily use nest boxes, a generous supply of nest boxes of various sizes can substitute for natural cavities when dead trees have been removed. Large numbers of bird boxes successfully sustain populations of pied flycatchers and other hole-nesting birds in highly managed European forests[4]. For example, installation of large numbers of boxes in two coniferous forests in southern Finland increased the total number of breeding pairs of pied flycatchers from 3 to 137 in one year.

Primary excavators are more difficult to accommodate when dead trees are absent. Chickadees will nest in boxes, particularly if the box is filled with sawdust so that they must excavate a cavity, but woodpeckers do not accept nest boxes. Alan Peterson and Thomas Grubb, Jr. have recently developed artificial snags in an attempt to provide alternative nest sites for woodpeckers[6] They use polystyrene "bead board" cylinders painted with brown latex enamel. The cylinders, which are about nine inches in diameter and eight feet tall, are supported by metal fence posts. Downy woodpeckers readily built roost cavities in the cylinders and some secondary cavity users (Carolina chickadees and house wrens) nested in some of these, but the woodpeckers did not use them for nesting. Woodpeckers tap near the nest entrance during courtship displays, so the absence of a resonant surface may have disrupted their breeding behavior. This could be easily rectified by placing a small strip of plywood near the top of the cylinder to serve as a sounding board[6] A potentially more serious problem is that a large number of cavities in the cylinders were damaged by raccoons, indicating that the bead board may not provide adequate protection from predators. With further refinement, however, artificial snags may provide alternative nest sites for woodpeckers. Eight-foot tall plastic cylinders might not fit well in every type of garden, but in some situations they could be hidden by landscaping.

Preserving Natural Diversity

Dead and dying trees are removed near houses because they are hazardous and are considered unsightly. Many people not only remove dying trees near the house, but also from woodlots to prevent the spread of insect pests and diseases to other trees. However, recent reports from the National Forest Service emphasize the importance of retaining large dead and dying trees to maintain populations of cavity-nesting birds[1] Most of these birds feed on bark and leaf insects, and they may play a major role in controlling populations of insects that attack trees[6]

Snags appear untidy if the primary esthetic criteria are neatness and symmetry. In the context of a more subtle esthetic judgment valuing natural diversity, a well-managed woodlot without dead trees is sterile and uninteresting. A dying or recently dead tree may be home to woodpecker nests and abandoned woodpecker holes inhabited by flying squirrels and nesting wrens and titmice. Later, as the dead wood rots, chickadees may dig a nest cavity and the base of the trunk may be decorated with bracket fungi. Even after the tree falls it will be rich with living things: delicate, ornate salamanders live under the fallen tree, while the moss-covered top is a rich seed bed for tree seedlings and herbs. The nutrients of the tree are returned to the humus or directly to other growing things. Rigorous removal of dead wood from a woodlot or large garden breaks this intricate cycle and reduces the diversity of living things. Naturalistic landscaping can result in a more complex and interesting environment than more formal landscape designs, and may even provide a place for weathered snags and the diverse group of birds and other animals that depend on dead wood. 🐦

Footnotes

1. Scott, V.E., K.E. Evans, D.R. Patton, and C.P. Stone. 1977. "Cavity-nesting birds of North American forests." Agricultural Handbook 511, Forest Service, U.S. Department of Agriculture.

2. DeGraaf, R.M. and A.L. Shigo. 1985. "Managing cavity trees for wildlife in the Northeast." General Technical Report NE-101, Northeastern Forest Experiment Station, Forest Service, U.S. Department of Agriculture.

3. Short, L.L. 1979. "Burdens of the picid hole-excavating habit." *Wilson Bulletin* 91: 16-28.

4. von Haartman, L. 1971. "Population dynamics," pp. 391-459 *in* D.S. Farner and J.R. King, eds., *Avian Biology,* volume 1, Academic Press, New York.

5. Askins, R.A. 1981. "Survival in winter: the importance of roost holes to resident birds." *The Loon* 53: 179-184.

6. Peterson, A.W. and T.C. Grubb, Jr. 1983. "Artificial trees as a cavity substrate for woodpeckers." *Journal of Wildlife Management* 47: 790-798.

A pair of house-hunting Eastern bluebirds finds a downy woodpecker excavating a cavity in a dead birch tree. In the distance tree swallows gather insects while on the wing. Other cavity nesters include the tree swallows, tufted titmice, white-breasted nuthatches, house wrens, and great crested flycatchers. Drawing by Julie Zickefoose

©1987 Zickefoose

Chemical Ecology of the Garden

Kurt E. Redborg

Think of the most bizarre, unusual way of earning a living that you possibly can; chances are there is some insect that is already doing just that. Nearly one million of these creatures have been described and new species are being discovered every day. One entomologist has speculated that the total number of insect species existing on this planet may be as high as 30 million! Insects can make a go of it in a rotting log, in a ball of dung, or in the minute area between the upper and lower epidermis of a plant leaf. The structural limitations imposed by their hardened armorlike exoskeletons demand that they be tiny—a blessing in disguise since insects can occupy environments unheard of for lumbering giants like ourselves. Changes in size necessitate periodic shedding of skin and secretion of a new and larger one. This miraculous ability to change their form is called metamorphosis. The next time you see some ugly-duckling of a caterpillar spin a cocoon, think of what it would be like to spend half your life as a human being, and half as some completely different creature.

One of the simplest ways for an insect to support its existence is by the tried and true method of eating plants. When insects invade our gardens or tree and shrub-filled yards, our interest in them may turn to irritation. However, the manner in which some insects locate their food provides an excellent example of the role of co-evolution between them and the plants on which they feed. Insects and higher plants have

evolved together, and over eons of time, the insects have developed clever ways of finding the tastiest, most suitable plant, for their ecological niche. Grasshoppers and gypsy moths locate their food by chance, and are not particular what it is. Squash beetles *(Diabrotica),* however, feed on any of the cucurbits, including pumpkins and melons. The plants of this family produce a bitter chemical compound which attracts the insects, and which does not seem to be of any other value to the plant. Changes in the genetic material in certain plants over time have caused the production of special compounds which are either attractive or repellent to the insect. These are called "allelochemics." Where the allelochemics repelled insects and thus protected the plants, the plants were able to expand their range and give rise to new species.

But the insects' genetic material and thus their chemistry can *also* change, and the insect can develop the ability to either neutralize or detoxify a plant poison. In this case, the insect will specialize in eating a particular group of plants, as the squash bugs do when they visit your melons. Chemical co-evolution between plants and insects is like a game of tag. The insect which became able to digest a poisonous plant toxin may be out of lunch if the plant chemistry changes yet again, and the new compound is toxic to the insect.

A chemical that was once a feeding deterrent may become an attractant, and a trigger for the insect to begin feeding. Insect mouth parts (maxillae) have hairlike receptors for tasting with incredible sensitivity. Some caterpillars can be induced to eat filter paper or other inedible material if it has been soaked with an extract of a plant which has a feeding stimulus; the hair receptors on the maxillae tell the insect to begin

Dr. Kurt E. Redborg is Assistant Professor of Zoology at Connecticut College. He is an entomologist trained at The University of Illinois who has served as director of educational services at the Thames Science Center in New London, Connecticut.

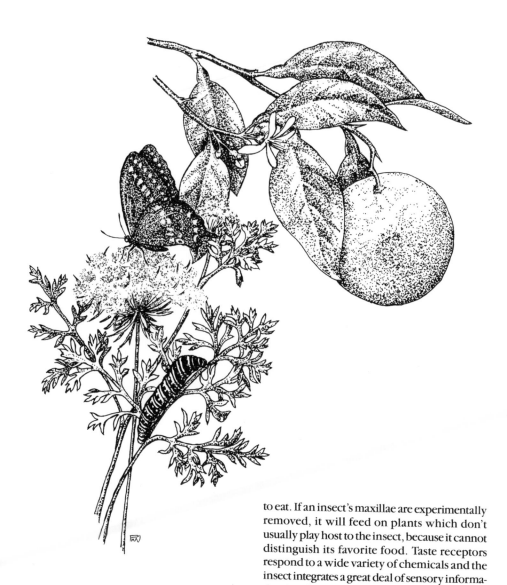

Plants of two different families, citrus at the top and parsley at the bottom, produce the same three essential oils that are attractive to the larvae of black swallowtail butterflies.

All drawings by Peter Nelson.

to eat. If an insect's maxillae are experimentally removed, it will feed on plants which don't usually play host to the insect, because it cannot distinguish its favorite food. Taste receptors respond to a wide variety of chemicals and the insect integrates a great deal of sensory information in selecting its "choice" of food.

Examples abound, including many that can be found in our own backyards. The tomato hornworm, the larval stage of a large Sphingid moth, feeds only on plants of the Solanaceae including tomato, eggplant, and pepper. Members of the family contain many alkaloid compounds, such as tomatine in tomato, which

*Cabbage worms feed on cabbage and will also
feed on nasturtiums which although not in the
mustard family do contain similar mustard oil
compounds.*

probably serve as feeding stimulants for the larvae. Plants such as cabbages, Brussels sprouts,
and radishes belong to the mustard family
(Cruciferae) and contain allelochemics known
as mustard oil glycosides which have been
shown to be egg-laying and feeding stimulants
for the cabbage white butterfly, *Pieris rapae.*
Most interesting is the fact that this butterfly will
also feed on the garden nasturtium which is not
a Crucifer but does contain similar mustard oil
compounds.

Some insects are definitely worth attracting
to your garden by growing the appropriate
plant. The black swallowtail, beautiful as both
a caterpillar and adult butterfly, can be attracted
to the garden with parsnip, parsley, dill, fennel,
and celery plants. These plants contain three
essential oils that are feeding stimulants for the
larvae. They will also feed on members of the
citrus family which contains the same three oils.
These chemical similarities between the parsnip
and citrus families suggests a closer evolution-
ary relationship between these families than had
been previously supposed. One might say that
the black swallowtail is a good taxonomic bot-
anist. When disturbed, the swallowtail larva
protrudes two bright orange scent horns which
exude an oily yellow secretion with an aniselike

like odor. As if to lend support to the adage "waste not, want not," the caterpillar has converted some of the plants' chemical substances into a defensive mechanism of its own.

The monarch butterfly is another insect that subverts plant chemicals to its own use. Cardiac glycosides, powerful poisons that affect vertebrate heart rate, are isolated by the larvae from the milkweed that they eat. Not only do these glycosides protect the plant from insect attack, they protect the larvae and adults of the monarch from attack by birds, because the insects poison the predator. The insects are brightly colored to advertise their distastefulness. One unpleasant encounter is usually enough to convince birds to "leave those orange and black butterflies alone." If you have milkweeds growing near the perimeter of your garden, consider leaving them as a source of attraction for these beautiful creatures.

Chemical ecology does not end with insects that eat plants. There are chemical cues for insects that eat insects that eat plants. Both the imported cabbage worm and the tomato hornworm are searched out by different species of small wasps belonging to the order Hymenoptera which lay their eggs within the body cavity. After hatching, the wasp larvae eat the caterpillar from the inside out. The caterpillar does not die until the very end, its vital organs having been consumed last. This bizarre form of predation, which sounds like it was made up for the plot of a science fiction movie, is termed *parasitoidism*. In the case of the hornworm, the parasitoid larvae burrow back out of the caterpillar and spin cocoons on its back, perhaps the final indignity. Like herbivores, parasitoids can be very host specific and locate their food by chemical signal. These signals could be plant substances emitted from injured plant tissue but they might be substances emitted from the plant eater itself, such as its chemical mating attractant or products associated with it such as frass or silk. One parasitoid may serve as a host for a secondary parasitoid which in turn may be attacked by yet another. The cecropia moth caterpillar, for instance, is at the beginning of a chain that includes no less than six different parasitoids.

As human beings we often tend to be somewhat chauvinistic and assume that other organisms perceive the world in the same way that we do. But the sensory energy that we respond to is only a small portion of the energy signals that are actually available to living organisms. The next time an insect flits through your garden, think of the chemical information bombarding its senses to which we are completely oblivious.

Milkweed provides the food for the larval stage of the monarch butterfly. The flowers are the source of nectar for the adult.

Plant a Garden for Beauty and the Butterflies

Maryanne Newsom-Brighton

Any gardener worth his or her tomatoes knows the horror of discovering an army of chomping caterpillars encamped in the cabbage patch. Yet one might argue in favor of caterpillars. After all, they mature into the wildly colored, delicate creations known as butterflies. And what gardener would not welcome the lovely butterflies!

America, long an advocate of wildlife plantings to attract birds and small animals, is now discovering plant management to encourage the fluttering gems of the insect world. Planting a butterfly garden is not a matter of sowing seeds which produce butterflies, but seeds whose plants will attract butterflies. Color, copious nectar and an "easy feed" are the three crucial requirements. Purple will catch a butterfly's attention first; yellow, pink and white are other favorites. Remember, too, butterflies need flowers with flat surfaces, clustered florets or large-lipped petals where they can perch comfortably while dining.

Monarch butterfly feeds on Joe-Pye Weed. Color plays a large part in attracting butterflies—in order of preference: purple, yellow, pink and white.

Swallowtail butterfly visits the brilliant orange flower clusters of butterfly weed (Asclepias tuberosa)—*a plant of the summer fields.*

Among the parade of flowering plants which attract butterflies two rank as the grand marshals. Butterfly weed *(Asclepias tuberosa)* is an orange milkweed of prairie regions. It prefers sandy, well-drained soil, but will readily naturalize in clay-based soils, providing tangerine-hued lunch counters for passing butterflies. *Buddleia*, or butterfly bush, a woody shrub, bears long spikes of pastel florets that resemble lilacs. Considered an evergreen in mild climates, the shrub dies back to the ground in winter elsewhere and comes back in early summer with new branches; flowers appear from late July until frost. Fritillaries, Swallowtails, Red Admirals and Painted Ladies will swarm to it.

Butterflies appear from early spring through late autumn, and a butterfly garden should be

Maryanne Newsom-Brighton is a freelance writer who lives in Indiana. Her seven-acre homestead is registered with the National Wildlife Federation as a backyard wildlife habitat, a project which has involved planting and landscaping to provide food, shelter, water and nesting sites for birds, bees, butterflies and animals.

planned to bloom accordingly. The earliest spring butterflies — Mourning Cloak, Tortoiseshell and Comma — are hibernators who have spent the winter in a dormant state. They eagerly cluster around early pussy willows *(Salix caprea)*, shrubs of damp areas which flower long before anything else has even thought about it. Of the cultivated spring-flowering butterfly choices, rock cress *(Arabis)*, lavender *(Lavandula)*, primrose *(Primula)*, purple rock cress *(Aubrieta)*, and Sweet William *(Dianthus barbatus)* are all sun-loving perennials. For mass plantings, short (six to ten inches) *Arabis*, *Aubrieta* and *Primula* make good borders as does the annual variegated candytuft *(Iberis)*, while taller lavender (two feet) fills in as a solid background plant. Primrose likes moist, acid soil, but Sweet William will tolerate a poor sandy growing medium. If space and time are limited, a lilac shrub *(Syringa)* is a carefree choice whose fragrant purple blooms will woo Swallowtail butterflies and human appreciation as well.

Warmer weather brings the Red Admiral, Painted Lady, Fritillary, Sulphur and Monarch butterflies. All can be tempted with such annuals as *Gaillardia* (blanket flower), heliotrope, mignonette, *Scabiosa* (pincushion

41

flower), and *Verbena*. Although heliotropes require well-drained rich soil to produce their lavender-hued, vanilla-scented flowers, both *Verbena* and *Gaillardia* thrive in sandy or poor soil, providing a flashy collage of multicolored blooms even during dry spells. For the "plant-it-once" gardener, perennials like butterfly weed (not the same as butterfly flower, *Schizanthus*), daisies and wild milkweed are easy-care butterfly bait. Of all the varieties of daisies, those with yellow centers or petals will lure the greatest numbers of nectar-sippers.

To meet the needs of the migrators and hibernators, nectar must be available until frost. Late summer/early fall butterfly choices are *Buddleia* (butterfly bush), *Phlox,* and *Sedum spectabile* (summer glory). Although there are numerous species of sedums, only the *Sedum spectabile* with its fleshy leaves and flat-topped dusty pink flowers is prized by butterflies.

If enough butterflies soar, float, flutter and cavort through one's garden, the inevitable result will be caterpillars, for the butterfly life cycle is a complete metamorphosis in four stages: egg, larva or caterpillar, pupa or chrysalis and adult. Most caterpillars are fussy eaters, finicky to the point of self-starvation if the proper food plant is not available. Luckily for the gardener, the majority of butterfly larvae prefer weeds over vegetables — milkweed for the Monarchs, clover for the Sulphurs, nettles for the Tortoiseshell and Red Admirals, thistle for the Painted Ladies, poplar and willow for the Mourning Cloaks.

Only the Fritillaries and Swallowtails sometimes munch themselves into trouble. Fritillary caterpillars relish passion vine and violets and can reduce the plants to shredded tatters. Swallowtail larvae feast on members of the Umbelliferae and, if the population gets out of hand, can decimate carrots, parsley, fennel and anise. However, the black-and-yellow striped chompers can be hand-picked and relocated on wild Queen Anne's lace where they will be just as happily nourished.

Butterflies suffer from habitat loss just like any other form of wildlife; their numbers hinge on the amount of food and territory available for both adults and larvae. A weedy patch in an out-of-the-way corner or an untended fence row can provide an excellent butterfly nursery with no maintenance, while a well-planned flower garden will benefit the adult insects. Additional "feeding stations" might take the form of bare patches of dry dirt baited with a bit of rotting fruit or dead fish.

Whether a butterfly garden is a single *Buddleia* shrub or massed beds of blooms, the neighborhood butterflies will soon locate them. The rewards are two-fold — not only showy blossoms swaying on green stems, but also fluttering bouquets of the flowers of the air.

Wing markings identify butterflies

Of the nearly 700 species of butterflies which flutter across the United States, a handful stand out as abundantly common and, luckily for most of us, readily discernable. Some, like the Mourning Cloak, are one-of-a-kind. Others have numerous variations—there are over 30 species of Fritillaries, for example—but their overall appearance is similar enough that the family is easily identified.

When you identify a butterfly, note the markings on both the upper and lower surfaces of the wings. A good field guide, such as the "Audubon Society Field Guide to North American Butterflies", is a valuable aid. Most of the butterflies described below occur in one form or another throughout North America.

Mourning Cloak looks like no other North American butterfly. The brownish maroon wings are bordered by a cream-colored band on the outer edge. Brilliant blue spots parallel the inner edge of the band. With a wingspan of two-and-seven-eights to three-and-three-eights inches, the Mourning Cloak is common throughout the U.S.

Tortoiseshell is distinguished by broad, ragged-edged wings which spread two-and-one-half to two-and-seven-eights inches. The wings are a rich, rust-brown near the body, blending to yellow-gold crescents at the outer margins. Somewhat particular in habitat, it dwells in the dense woodlands and along river courses in Canada south to Oregon, Colorado, Minnesota and the mountains of Missouri and South Carolina.

Comma can be found from eastern Colorado to the Atlantic coast, south to Georgia. The Comma is a rust-brown color with black blotches; the hind wings are marked with a broad dark margin. The most distinctive mark is the silver backward C on the underneath side of the hind wing.

Swallowtail is a large, brightly colored but-

Newly emerged black swallowtail butterfly rests above parsley plants—a favorite food of the caterpillar.

terfly with "tails" on the hind wings. Some variety of Swallowtail is found in every part of the U.S. The three most familiar Swallowtails are the Tiger (yellow with black striping across the wings), the Zebra (white with black stripes and a swordlike tail), and the Black (black and blue-black with yellow, orange and/or cream spots on wing rim.)

Sulphur loves open country, meadows and parks anywhere in the U.S. except Florida. It is a smaller butterfly (wingspan 1¼ to 2 inches) in some shade of yellow or yellowish-green. The Sulphurs keep their wings closed when feeding or resting.

Fritillary is generally dull orange with black blotches on the upper side. The underside of the wings looks like a checkerboard of silver, white or yellow spots edged in black. Fritillaries appear to have only four legs instead of six because the forelegs are vestigial and nearly use-less. Some variety of Fritillary inhabits every part of North America.

Red Admiral is most easily recognized by the orange-red bars which cross the front wings and border the hind wings; it looks like a huge orange "U" was stamped on the black butterfly. Red Admirals are common from subarctic Canada to Central America.

Painted Lady is also known as Cosmopolite and considered by some to be the most widespread butterfly in the world. The upper side of the wings is gold near the body, blending to salmon-orange, then black on the wingtips. The underside of the wings is patterned in white, blue, olive and brown with an orange streak under the front wings.

Monarch migrated across all of North America except through Alaska and the Pacific Northwest coast. It is characterized by its brilliant orange wings with their black veins and black margins sprinkled with white dots. 🦋

A Garden Fit for Hummingbirds

Maryanne Newsom-Brighton

DON'T MOVE," my husband whispered, across the irises. As I waited, motionless, I heard a buzzing, punctuated by high-pitched squeaks, right behind me. Turning slowly I found myself nose-to-bill with a ruby-throated hummingbird that was investigating my red shirt. We stared at each other a few seconds, the bird and I. Then, apparently satisfied that my blouse was *not* some strange new flower, the "hummer" sped off to sample the nearby columbines.

Such encounters are common in our garden. The hummingbirds whizzing by sometimes unnerve visitors, but apprehension quickly gives way to fascination. Delicate, fearless, and quick as lightning, hummingbirds have charmed and amazed people for centuries. Ask anyone who has ever hung out a red-tinted sugar-water feeder in hopes of enticing the bird that Audubon admiringly called "a glittering fragment of the rainbow."

Syrup may appeal to the hummer's sweet tooth, but it does not provide all the nourishment required by the quarter-ounce bird. The serious hummingbird watcher needs to plant a garden. Hummingbirds feed every 10 to 15 minutes from dawn to sunset, often consuming more than half their weight in food and eight times their weight in water per day. One male Anna's hummingbird requires the nectar from 1,000 fuchsia blossoms to maintain his metabolism for a single day. Hummingbird gardeners, remember: Plant plenty.

The ideal hummingbird plant is red, orange, or pink and has either large, solitary flowers or loosely clustered blossoms that often droop.

The typically tubular flowers hold copious reservoirs of nectar at the base of a long, stout floral tube and frequently have protruding stamens or pistils. Scent is unimportant, for hummers depend on sight rather than smell. Red flowers usually contrast sharply with the surrounding vegetation, although in the Southwest, where much of the landscape is brown, greenish flowers are a beacon to hummingbirds. Fledglings learn by trial and error to seek out tubed nectar flowers, most of which are red. The youngsters soon link red with food. So strong is the association that throughout their lives hummingsbirds boldly investigate every new source of red—roses, bandanas, neckties, even the insulators on electric fences.

The birds are belligerent and territorial, and some will tirelessly defend every food source in sight. For this reason, hummingbird plantings for more than one bird should be separated. The prized perch in our yard is a utility wire between house and garage. From there the dominant hummingbird—we call him the Baron—commands a view of a salvia bed, four-o'clocks, a buddleia, jewelweed, red-hot pokers (*Kniphofia* species), and even our sugar-water feeder. He sends intruders packing amid a flurry of flashing wings and avian expletives. Thus far the Baron has evicted butterflies, northern orioles, and a chipmunk—not to mention countless other hummers. We have outsmarted him by

Reprinted courtesy of *Horticulture, The Magazine of American Gardening,* 755 Boylston St., Boston, MA 02116. ©1986, Horticulture Partners

adding a border of scarlet sage to the backyard, where other hummers can feed out of the Baron's view. (Blooms that lack a landing platform will discourage competition from bees and butterflies.)

When choosing plants, consider species whose bloom dates overlap, thus supplying a continuous source of nectar. Among the flowers most popular with both hummingbirds and gardeners are the scarlet sage (*Salvia splendens*), nasturtium (*Tropaeolum majus*), and four-o'clock (*Mirabilis jalapa*). Salvias bloom from early summer until frost, generally thriving in full sun, although partial shade may be necessary in the South. They lend themselves to bedding and range from eight-to ten-inch dwarfs to three-foot-high cultivars. Nasturtiums

Flowering crabapples (below, a tea crab) Malus *spp. offer spring color and clustered blossoms, attracting hummingbirds.*
Photo by Gottscho-Schleisner, Inc.

thrive on neglect in dry, infertile soil and full sun but tend to be at their best in cool weather. If space is limited, try a hybrid nasturtium bred for climbing a trellis or hanging from a basket, like 'Fordhook's Favorite'.® Steer clear of double-flowered varieties; their nectar cache is not as obvious or as accessible to hummers.

Toss the four-o'clock seeds in the garden and forget them. They sprout readily, bloom profusely, and true to their name, open their red, yellow and white blossoms in late afternoon, earlier on cloudy days. Four-o'clocks tolerate dust, soot, fumes, and other airborne particles of pollutants. Allow four-o'clocks plenty of room, and be prepared to enjoy them for years to come, as they reseed themselves with enthusiasm. Three years ago I converted one bed of salvia to four-o'clocks, just for that summer—or so I thought. But each spring volunteer four-o'clocks crowd out whatever else I plant there. I'm not thrilled, but Baron thinks the results are grand and jealously guards that

Butterfly bush (Buddleia davidii) *has either purple, pink, blue or white flowers. Insects and spiders provide much of hummingbirds' diets and are often snatched from this plant.*

Photo by Gottscho-Schleisner, Inc.

particular bed from his perch on the electric line.

Hummingbirds inhabitat nearly all of the United States, although they are rare in the Great Plains, and only in the Sun Belt—Florida through Texas and the Southwest— do they reside year-round. Elsewhere they merely summer, and flee south with the approach of cold weather. Spring migrants usually return with the blossoming of their favorite nectar plants. A cool, damp spring may delay the flowers but not the birds. Our southern-Indiana hummers arrive the first week of May regardless of the weather, and some years early-blooming quince and sugar-water feeders are crucial to their survival until the flower season is in full swing. Tardy autumn stragglers are just as vulnerable, depending on late bloomers like red sage and jewelweed, plus a still-full sugar-water feeder, for a successful migration.

Although the ruby-throated is the only species of hummingbird east of the Mississippi, the region west of the Great Plains and on to the Pacific Coast hosts at least seven common species and a few other casual visitors who stray north from Mexico. I have seen a broad-tailed hummingbird high in Colorado's Rocky Mountains and a rufous hummingbird along the Alaskan coast. Calliope, Anna's, black-chinned,

Costa's, and Allen's hummingbirds round out the western roster

The hummingbird's favorite flowers of the West, painted cups or Indian paintbrushes (*Castilleja* species), are wildlings not suited to transplanting. However, the century plant (*Agave americana*) will make any western garden a four-star restaurant for a hummingbird, as will scarlet gilia (*Gilia* species), trumpet honeysuckle (*Lonicera sempervirens*), and tree tobacco (*Nicotiana glauca*). Red-flowering gooseberry (*Ribes speciosum*) and red-flowering currant (*Ribes sanguineum*) draw a crowd in West Coast gardens.

In recent years Taylor Herb Gardens of Vista, California, has introduced ruby, golden, and amethyst "hummingbird flowers." The ruby flower, pineapple-scented sage (*Salvia elegans*), and the amethyst, Mexican-bush sage (*Salvia leucantha*), are shrubby natives of Mexico, where they grow four to six feet high. The golden hummingbird flower, better known as lion's ear (*Leonotis leonurus*), is from South Africa and was once used medicinally. All three love sun, tolerate poor soil, and bloom all summer. "We maintain a six-foot-thick hedge of them," says Kent Taylor, "and the hummingbirds swarm over them to the exclusion of everything else." Taylor points out that his hummingbird flowers are perennial in the South and Southwest, but in colder climates they must be cut back, potted, and over-wintered indoors or treated as annuals.

Gardeners in the Southeast may want to plant a mimosa tree (*Albizia julibrissin*) to please the ruby-throated hummingbirds. Other tropical plants for hummers include scarlet bush (*Hamelia erecta*), royal poinciana (*Delonix regia*), a scarlet mallow (*Hibiscus coccineus*), purple cestrum (*Cestrum purpureum*), and the yellow-flowering lantana (*Lantana camara*).

Many hummingbird watchers supplement their flower offerings with sugar-water feeders. A solution of one part sugar to four parts water is recommended. Anything stronger is considered too sweet—although the birds themselves might disagree. Bring the solution to a boil, turn off the heat, and allow it to cool. Coloring is not necessary; with all the controversy over red dyes for human consumption, why take a chance on hummingbirds? Sugar solutions must be kept fresh. Honey is definitely a "no-no," as it is easily contaminated and subject to souring, fermentation, and bacterial growth.

Sugar-water feeders are available at most garden centers, feed stores that carry wild-bird seed, and specialty mail-order companies. Buy a feeder that is easy to clean and holds several ounces. One of my early purchases was a two-ounce vial; I found myself running out to refill it twice a day. My present feeder holds a cup, but at the season's peak I'm lucky if it lasts two days.

Sheer speed (hummingbirds have been unofficially clocked at around 30 mph) keeps a hummingbird safe from capture, but other perils are not so easily avoided. Feeders and plantings too near a window invite crashes, especially when quarreling birds become rambunctious. Pesticides are a great danger. A surprising por-

tion of the tiny birds' diet consists of insects and spiders. Hummingbirds snatch some in midair; they procure others from plum, cherry, apricot, and orange blossoms, as well as thistle, *Buddleia*, and the other nectar-rich blooms. Indiscriminate use of insecticides destroys insects vital to hummingbirds and coats the flowers themselves, endangering the lives of the beautiful creatures that feed on them.

Occasionally gardeners unknowingly prune off nest-bearing branches. Hummingbirds make thimble-sized nests, about an inch across, and camouflage them with spider webs, bud scales, and lichens. They frequently nest on small, down-sloping limbs near or over water. You might locate the nest by watching where the female goes when she leaves the feeder. The safest practice, though, is to hang up the pruning shears until the fledglings appear at the flower beds. 🐦

The tubular flowers of honeysuckle (below, Lonicera japonica) *hold quantities of nectar, hungrily sought by many species of hummingbirds.*

Photo by Gottscho-Schleisner, Inc.

Seeing Red: Plants for a Hummingbird Garden

The plants listed below are among hummingbirds' favorites. While reds dominate the list, there are plenty of other colors suggested to allow a varied planting. The most important aspect of designing a hummingbird garden is to plan for continuous bloom from spring to fall, ensuring an endless supply of nectar.

Common Name	Latin Name	Annual Biennial Perennial	Bloom Dates	Color	Soil Requirements	Sun	Useful Range
Flowers:							
Bee balm	Monarda didyma	P	July-August	red, pink	not particular	◑	zones 4-9
Bleeding heart	Dicentra spectabilis	P	May-June	rose	rich, well-drained	◑	3-9
Butterfly weed	Asclepias tuberosa	P	July-August	orange	tolerates most soils; thrives in dry, sandy sites	○	3-9
Cardinal flower	Lobelia cardinalis	P	July-frost	red	moist	○ ◑	5-9
Carpet bugle	Ajuga reptans	P	May-June	blue, purple	—	● ◑	4-9
Columbines	Aquilegia spp.	P	May-June	red, pink, yellow, blue, white	rich, well drained	○ ◑	3-9, depending on species
Coralbells	Heuchera sanguinea	P	June-September	red	moist, well-drained	○ ◑	3-9
Dahlia	Dahlia merckii	A or P (tender bulb)	July-frost	red, pink, orange, yellow, white	rich, well-drained	○ ◑	2-10
Delphinium or scarlet larkspur	Delphinium cardinale	P	June-frost	red	rich, well-drained	○ ◑	6-9
Four-o'clock	Mirabilis jalapa	A or P depending on climate	July-frost	red, rose, pink, cream, white	tolerates dry soil	○	4-10
Foxglove	Digitalis purpurea	P or B	June-July	purple, red, rose, cream, white	fertile	○ ◑	4-9
Fuchsia	Fuchsia 'Riccartonii'	A or P	July-frost	red	—	◑	6-10
Gladioli	Gladiolus spp.	A or P (tender bulb)	July-September	many colors	fertile	○	—
Jewelweed	Impatiens capensis	A	June-frost	orange	moist	● ◑	5-9
	Impatiens pallida	A	June-frost	yellow	moist	● ◑	5-9
Nasturtiums	Tropaeolum majus	A	June-frost	scarlet, orange, yellow, white	tolerates dry, infertile soil	○	—
Penstemons or beard-tongues	Penstemon spp.	P	June-July	purple, scarlet, pink, yellow	acidic	○ ◑	5-9, depending on species
Petunias	Petunia spp.	A	early summer-frost	many colors	loamy	○ ◑	—
Phlox	Phlox drummondii	A	July-August	many colors	tolerates dry soil	○ ◑	—
	Phlox spp.	P	July-frost	many colors		○ ◑	2-8 depending on species
Red-hot poker or tritoma	Kniphofia uvaria	P	July-August	red, yellow	moist, sandy	○	6-10
Sage	Salvia officinalis	A or P	midsummer	lavender	—	○	5-10
Sage, scarlet	Salvia splendens	A or P, depending on climate	July-frost	red	—	○	4-10
Snapdragon	Antirrhinum majus	A	June	red, pink, white	rich, slightly alkaline	○ ◑	—

Common Name	Latin Name	Annual Biennial Perennial	Bloom Dates	Color	Soil Requirements	Sun	Useful Range
Flowers:							
Spider flower	*Cleome spinosa*	A	August-September	rose, pink, white	any dry soil	○	—
Sweet William	*Dianthus barbatus*	A or B	May-June	red, maroon, rose, pink, white	—	○	3-8
Tobacco, flowering	*Nicotiana alata*	A or P	June-August	many colors	moist, fertile	○ ◐	perennial in the South
Zinnias	*Zinnia spp.*	A	July-frost	many colors	—	○	—
Vines:							
Honeysuckle, trumpet	*Loincera sempervirens*	P	June-frost	red	moist	○	3-9
	Loincera beckrottii	P	June-frost	red and yellow	moist	○	3-9
Morning glory	*Ipomoea coccinea*	A	July-frost	red	not too rich	○	3-10
	Ipomoea purpurea	A	July-frost	purple to blue	not too rich	○	3-10
Scarlet runner bean	*Phaseolus coccineus*	A or P	July-frost	red	—	○	not frost hardy
Trumpet creeper	*Campsis radicans*	P	July-September	orange, red	rich	○	5-9
Shrubs:							
Azaleas	*Rhododendron spp.*		late May-June	red, pink, white	rich, acidic, well-drained	◐	2-8 depending on species
Beauty bush	*Kolkwitzia amabilis*		May-June	pink	well-drained	○ ◐	4-9
Butterfly bush	*Buddleia davidii*		July-September	purple, pink, blue, white	well-drained	○	5-9
Coralberry	*Symphoricarpos orbiculatus*		June	pink, white	—	○ ◐	4-9
Flowering currant	*Ribes odoratum*		May-June	rose, yellow	—	◐	4
Hardy fuchsia	*Fuchsia magellanica*		June	violet and red	moist, well-drained	○ ◐	6-8, with protection
Tatarian honeysuckle	*Lonicera tatarica*		May-June	red, pink	tolerates poor soil	○	3-9
Flowering quince	*Chaenomeles japonica*		April-May	red	—	○	4-9
Rose of Sharon	*Hibiscus syriacus*		July-August	pink, white	moist, well-drained	○ ◐	5-9
Weigela	*Weigela florida*		May-June	red, maroon, pink	—	○ ◐	5-9
Trees:							
Buckeye or horse-chestnut	*Aesculus glabra*		May	yellow to white	moist	○ ◐	3-8
Buckeye, red	*Aesculus carnea*		May	red	moist	○ ◐	8-9
Horse-chestnut	*Aesculus hippocastanum*		May	yellow to white	moist	○	3-8
Black locust	*Robinia pseudoacacia*		May	white	well-drained	○	2-10
Chinaberry	*Melia azedarach*		April	purple to lilac	well-drained	○	7-10
Flowering crabs	*Malus spp.*		April-May, depending on species	red, rose, pink, white	—	○	4-8, depending on species

Common Name	Latin Name	Bloom Dates	Color	Soil Requirements	Sun	Useful Range
Hawthorns	*Crataegus spp.*	April-May, depending on species	red, rose, white	tolerates neutral or poor soil	○	4-8, depending on species
Mimosa, silk tree	*Albizia julibrissin*	July-August	pink	tolerates poor, dry soil	○	6-9
Siberian pea tree	*Caragana arborescens*	May-June	yellow	well-drained	◑	2-9
Tulip poplar	*Liriodendron tulipifera*	May-June	yellow with orange markings	moist, well-drained	◑	4-9

*Blooming times may vary from one region to the next.
 These dates are given to suggest duration and sequence of bloom.

○ = sun
◑ = partial sun or shade
● = shade

Ed. note: The zones apply to the USDA climate zone map.

Trumpet vine provides summer color and food for many hummingbards.

The Rose Plant Ecosystem.

A rose plant produces leaf, flower, fruit and seed.
Every part of it is eaten by primary consumers.
They are eaten in turn by secondary consumers,
who are eaten by tertiary consumers.

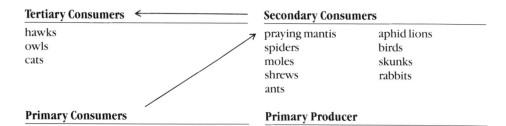

Tertiary Consumers ← ——————————— **Secondary Consumers**

hawks
owls
cats

praying mantis   aphid lions
spiders   birds
moles   skunks
shrews   rabbits
ants

Primary Consumers **Primary Producer**

Pollinators
bees
flying insects

Leaf Feeders
garden snail
Japanese beetle
leaf-cutter bees
caterpillars
leaf rollers

Root Feeders
weevils
grubs
nematodes

Sucking Insects
white flies
leaf hoppers
aphids

Rosa 'Lotte Gunthart'

Birds ——————————→ **Fruit**
cedar waxwings   seeds
mockingbirds
mice

ON THE WATERFRONT

Noble Proctor

I f you are lucky enough to move into a house with a river frontage, or a lake or decent-sized pond at the foot of the garden, spend some time watching what happens before planning any changes. Find out which water-side plants are growing there and which birds are using them for food or shelter. Large areas of reeds or so-called "bulrushes" may extend right across your frontage, and it is perhaps tempting to clear them away to give a clear view across areas of open water—but it may be much better to create a couple of large gaps in the cover, retaining some of it at either end and in a clump or two in the middle. This broken edge effect is likely to prove more attractive to more bird species than either a clear shoreline or a continuous, unbroken line of vegetation. By producing little bays and inlets you will provide loafing spots for duck, feeding areas for snipe and open crossing points which might help you to spot more furtive birds like the Virginia rail. You might also attract a heron and, if you provide one or two strategically placed perches, regular visits from a kingfisher.

If you are fortunate enough to have a long frontage on to a lake, it could pay dividends to think in terms of creating a length of irregular shoreline, with miniature bays, promontories and shallows. This will probably involve you in many hours' manual labor, but the chance of attracting more waterfowl and perhaps migrant waders like solitary and spotted sandpipers will make it very worthwhile. A big post in the water will also be useful as a perching place for a number of birds.

In upland areas, some gardens back on to rocky or fast-moving streams, where spotted sandpipers, and in the west, dippers, may all occur as breeding birds. Generally, it is not possible to manage the foot of your garden to attract these species, although a contrived bit of grav-

Reprinted from GARDEN BIRDS © 1986 by Rodale Press, Inc. Permission granted by Rodale Press, Inc., Emmaus, PA 18049.

Ponds create an area that will attract a variety of wildlife. Here the turtles line up to enjoy the sun.
Photo by Joseph Sweeney — BBG.

A green heron perches upon a label in BBG's lily pools. He is an expert fisherman and awaits an easy catch.
Photo by Slim Zumwalt — BBG.

Female mallard and her young rest on the center of a small pool containing a variety of aquatic plants.
Photo: Brooklyn Botanic Garden

elly shore might help sandpipers and a garden pond should certainly attract green herons. If there is none in place already, it would be worth positioning a couple of large, round-topped stones in the water where you can see them. All these birds will find them and use them—dippers may pause to feed in the eddies around them.

One final point concerning water frontages: a relatively swift-moving lowland stream may provide you with the opportunity of growing your own cress if you have the room to divert the water across a shallow area. This leads not only to good eating, but produces excellent conditions for a number of birds, including pipits and even warblers.

In addition, shallow water areas may also

serve to attract small numbers of hawks who relish shallow water in which they like to bathe.

Water for birds

Most people, of course do not have rivers, streams, lakes or ponds at the foot of their gardens, but for many bird gardeners the provision of water is often one of their first considerations. Birds need water to survive; you can provide it quite easily, either as a simple drinking or bathing supply, or in the form of a man-made pond.

Birdbaths are available in a variety of forms, either on pedestals or as precast or molded mini-pools for placing at ground level. All of these are perfectly acceptable to birds, but you can just as easily make your own, using an upturned trashcan lid or a small sheet of heavy gauge pond-liner. If you do make your own, remember to give the birds easy access from gently sloping sides, or via a brick or stone placed in the water. Remember that shallow water is all that is needed; keep it clean of leaves

Noble Proctor is Professor of Ornithology at Southern Connecticut State University. He has written several books and leads bird tours around the world. He recently won the Connecticut Conservationist Award.

and debris and change the water regularly.

Water is important in winter and, even if you do not maintain a year-round supply for your birds, you should endeavor to provide it in hard weather. The problem is, of course, that water freezes easily—so what is to be done? *On no account* should you add any form of anti-freezing substance to the water: the chances are that it will do some harm to the birds. You can, of course, adopt the irksome course of going out and breaking the ice regularly, or adding warm water at intervals, but nowadays most people think instead of installing a simple heater to maintain the water temperature above freezing point. An aquarium heater, available at any good pet store, does the job perfectly well but it will, of course, require external, weatherproof wiring—a local electrician should be able to advise you on this aspect. If you are putting water out in a shallow container, for example a trashcan lid, it is very effective to raise the whole affair on bricks and place a simple nightlight in the space underneath it.

Making a pond
Making an artificial pond is an exciting prospect (at least it is once you've dug the hole). This is in any case a popular and common practice among gardeners, and many of the better gardening books give excellent advice on what to do. A formal garden pool—even a fairly sophisticated water garden—will provide good conditions for birds, but in many ways a purpose-built pool is better. The only constraints are how much you want to spend and how much space you have available.

Broadly speaking, the aim is to produce a pond with a slightly irregular outline, shallow at the edges (or at least at one end) and not more that 3 ¼ ft deep in any place. It should provide "walk-in" access to birds and easily accessible drinking and bathing places. Through a mixture of native and more exotic plants, it can be both visually attractive and a good source of food for birds. A pool can be designed in conjunction with another garden feature—an adjacent rock garden perhaps. This could also provide a simple waterfall system whereby water is pumped up and returned to the pond by gravity, producing oxygenation which is essential for a successful and productive pond. The alternative is to stock the pool with plenty of oxygenating plants, hornwort, for example.

A heavy clay soil provides a ready-made pond-liner which will cost you nothing other than a lot of sweat and toil. But soils with good drainage require entirely artificial techniques for which there are three alternatives. It is possible nowadays to purchase quite large, molded glass fiber ponds which are excellent for the small garden. Their major disadvantage is that the size and shape is predetermined by the manufacturers. Preparing a concrete lining, and coating it with plastic paint, gives you much greater flexibility, but is laborious and, once completed, very difficult to alter in any significant way. A better alternative is to line your excavation with heavy-duty plastic sheeting, which is no more expensive than the other methods and is much more flexible in design terms.

At all stages of construction, extreme care must be taken not to damage or puncture the sheeting. It is important to provide a reasonably smooth base on which to lay the sheeting and then to lay it generously, to allow for its movement and settling when soil is placed upon it, and again when you add the weight of the water. Allow a wide overlap at the edges and do not trim off the surplus until the whole pond is completed and filled. Again, be very careful not to damage the sheeting if any large stones, plant containers etc. are to rest on it.

Rainwater would eventually fill your pool, but it is better and faster to do it from the tap, using a hose pipe. Add a few buckets of water from a local pond to help introduce the first micro-organisms to the new environment. Allow the water to settle for about two weeks (topping up the level if necessary) before any planting is undertaken. The layer of soil you have placed on the pond-liner will provide most of what you need for planting, but plants in containers can also be placed as required; use some of the soil from the excavation to build up a low surround to incorporate the overlap of the sheeting and to provide a good moisture-retaining base for waterside plants.

Stocking the pond

Many of the plants available commercially for garden ponds will be suitable, but, for a more natural look, a much better strategy is to introduce a majority of natural species—the sort of things that grow in real ponds in your area. However, the law places certain restraints on the uprooting of wild plants, even common ones. Be sure that you have the necessary permission before going to your local pond for supplies; take only a few plants of the kinds you need and cause as little damage as possible while doing so. Choose only places where these plants are abundant. In many ways, it is often better to scrounge what you want from neighbors or friends with established ponds. As already mentioned, hornwort is an excellent oxygenating plant. Some other useful species you can introduce include water mint, water forget-me-not, water plantain, marsh marigold, mare's tail, yellow or blue flag iris, bogbean, purple loosestrife, frogbit (floating), amphibious bistort (floating) and (at the deepest parts) water lilies. Cattail *(Typha)* will grow well around the wet edges, as will bog arum, primulas and various ferns. The cattails will form big, attractive stands and may need some control as your pond matures. Unless you have a lot of room or are prepared to carry out continuous management it is probably not a good idea to introduce the highly invasive and fast-spreading common reed *(Phragmites)*.

There is a good chance that the American toad (and perhaps newts) will colonize unaided—but here, too, you can ask a friend or neighbor for spawn or tadpoles from a well-established pond. A supply of the spawn of the American frog could be even more valuable. This has become a scarce animal in some areas, and founding a new, protected colony could be an important local conservation project. Remember that both frogs and toads require easy access into and out of the pond—gently sloping banks or strategically placed stones will help them. They also like flat stones placed in the water, both at and just under the surface. During hot weather watch for falling water levels and adjust the exits accordingly.

Bird gardeners will welcome visits by kingfishers and green herons, but the latter can be unpopular in gardens where ponds are stocked with goldfish and other ornamental species. Netting over the water is an effective way to stop predation, while erecting simple string or wire lines around the edge of the pool can also be an effective deterrent. Model heron or heron-like birds often make gardeners groan with distaste, but they, too, can prove quite effective deterrents in the short term. Fortunately, green heron predation tends to be rather seasonal, at least in garden ponds, usually involving mainly young birds in the late summer and fall."

A Wildlife Garden in Newfoundland

Jane Power

The nature reserve of the Memorial University Botanical Garden, Oxen Pond, Newfoundland, has been designed to encourage flora and fauna in a balanced ecosystem. As you enter the reserve, you encounter a sun-exposed rough meadow, constantly maintained to discourage the pioneer growth of trees and shrubs. Sheltered from Newfoundland's prevailing winds by encompassing multiflora rose, native red elderberry and coniferous woodlands, this habitat provides an ideal environment for small mammals, birds and insects.

Wildflowers such as lance-leaved goldenrod, black knapweed and pearly everlasting, along with some grass species, offer favorite host and nectar sources for butterflies and other pollinating insects. Throughout the fall and winter months, birdfeeders are replenished daily, if need be, and are frequently visited by blue jays, black-capped and boreal chickadees, slate-colored juncos, purple finches, evening grosbeaks and the occasional flicker. Bird boxes provide sanctuary for tree swallows and chickadees in the spring and summer. Bordering the coniferous woodlot are bat boxes, designed to attract Newfoundland's more common bat species, the insectivorous little brown bat.

Not much further along, a habitat simulating a woodland glade is managed primarily for butterflies. The herbaceous plants cow parsnip, scotch lovage and angelica have been introduced as hosts for the caterpillars of the short-tailed swallowtail; while the woody plants chuckley-pear, pin cherry, choke cherry and a self-seeded apple tree provide food for the caterpillars of the Canadian tiger swallowtail and white admiral butterflies.

Patches of lance-leaved goldenrod have been located where the sun hits them at different times of the day, thus ensuring that nectar is available for as many hours as possible. This native wildflower is one of the best known nectar sources for late summer butterflies; at least 11 species have been observed using it in Newfoundland. Twenty-six butterfly species have been recorded in the Memorial University Botanical Garden; some have not been seen anywhere else in Newfoundland.

A woodpile, one of the many throughout the Garden, is especially constructed to provide shelter for overwintering butterflies and refuge for snowshoe hare and other small mammals. Felt, in the surface layer of the woodpile, assists in keeping the interior dry.

Wildlife gardens inspire and educate. Here student, artist and gardener may enrich their knowledge of the natural world. 🦋

Cardinals are regular visitors to feeding stations. Their favorite food is sunflower seeds. At left, Northern Cardinal.

MUSKRATS

Cathy Walker

Muskrats have been one of the most destructive pests at the Chicago Botanic Garden.*

They are large water rodents with brown fur and webbed feet.

Muskrats will feed on just about anything. Our water garden was completely destroyed by them the year it was installed. Leaves of the water lilies and lotus were chewed but they primarily fed on the submerged tubers. Any plant in the water or near the water's edge is considered to be in danger of muskrat damage. They have chewed off young branches of shrubs, tender bark of trees (girdling them) and tree and shrub roots growing near the water. Once, they undermined and ate an entire bed of bulbs that was adjacent to the lagoon. *Iris pseudacoris, I. versicolor, Juncus spp.* and *Pontederia cordata* were the only plants not readily eaten but when all other food was gone the muskrats would feed on them too! They can be seen feeding at any time during the day.

The muskrats live in burrows along the shoreline. They burrow under trees and shrubs creating air pockets. When the roots of nearby vegetation grow into their tunnels they quickly dry out and are killed. Almost all of the trees and large bed areas at the garden are tiled and drain directly into the lagoon. These drainage tiles make a perfect pre-constructed home for the muskrats.

Our Plant Protection Department has been working in cooperation with the Illinois Department of Conservation to try to minimize our muskrat population. Underwater traps were set beneath the ice during the winter months. Live traps set along the shoreline can be used but catching the muskrats is more difficult as they do not like to come out of the water.

For additional protection in the water garden, the tubers of the water plants were covered with one inch square galvanized wire mesh screen. The mesh screen provides a physical barrier that the rodents cannot get under while the plants are able to grow through it.

The muskrat is an aquatic rodent with brown fur and a long scaly tail. It is about the size of a small cat and lives in holes or mounds of rushes, brush and mud at pond's edges.

Ed. note: The Chicago Botanic Garden is made up of nine islands surrounded by 60 acres of water.

Cathy Walker is a Horticulture Information Specialist at the Chicago Botanic Garden, Glencoe, Illinois.

Urban Gardens
Attract Wildlife

Barbara Pesch

Homeowners and apartment dwellers with little area to landscape need not despair. It is amazing to observe what wildlife will be attracted to urban areas where there are plantings of window boxes, barrels and small pools.

In a relatively small space on a 17th-floor terrace, I have had the good fortune to attract a surprising variety of wildlife. My plantings are all in containers—from boxes to barrels. In an old wine barrel I grow a water lily and this small garden pool attracts many birds for its water. An upright yew *(Taxus* sp.*),* Japanese black pine *(Pinus thunbergiana)* and purple-leaved plum *(Prunus cerasifera* 'Atropurpurea') occupy other large barrels. Geraniums, petunias, blue lobelia, impatiens and assorted houseplants cascade from pots and planters.

This urban terrace garden has been visited by four species of butterflies at regular intervals. Bees are also constant visitors. Birds have of course included pigeons, as well as house finches, blue jays, a wandering warbler or two and several kestrals. Other visitors to the terrace include a praying mantis (a miracle of sorts) and several squirrels. I try to discourage the latter as they are bent on digging up all my plants. But they are determined—the trip to my terrace is a 17-story climb along a fire escape!

The look of a window box in an urban setting can be its own reward. However, when the possibility of a passing butterfly or two is added (and perhaps even a hummingbird), the visual delights multiply enormously. Personally, I feel that attracting wildlife in densely populated New York is an exciting challenge. 🦋

SUBURBAN WILDLIFE

Sally Taylor

How do we coexist with suburban wildlife in our gardens? Last spring when I went out to exult over the progress of my three year evergreen ground cover planting of different North Tisbury hybrid azaleas, fate and rabbits had played a cruel joke on me. There was not a single flower or leaf bud left on the tips of the low-growing woody stems. Each one had been neatly removed, with the slanting cut from a rodent. My heart sank, because I had not known that we had rabbits or woodchucks living on our land. Last winter was difficult, with an unusual amount of snow cover, lasting nearly to the middle of March. As the snow melted, the projecting shoots of the azaleas were delectable targets for a rabbit repast, for it was indeed a rabbit we saw coming back to the free lunch several days later.

These North Tisbury hybrids are part of a planting of small or low-growing rhododendrons, extending along a raised bed. Small plants of *Rhododendron* 'Dora Amateis' and *R. racemosum* were untouched. We devised a low cage of chicken wire bent to cover the whole plant, and by fall new growth had appeared on all the cut stems. We lost a year's growth of buds and flowers, however, and this next season will see a low two-foot chicken wire fence around the azalea garden. The fine chicken wire is next to invisible, and is sufficient to deter the rabbits.

Another planting which the rabbits enjoyed was the ground cover three-leaved cinquefoil *(Potentilla fruticosa)*. This also is a low-growing evergreen, and like other members of the rose family, attractive to rabbits. By midsummer, the cinquefoil had recovered, and in fact prospered from having a short haircut. By now, the clover in the lawn had become the lunch counter.

Woodchucks also arrived this year, and their specialty was the emerging day lilies, followed by new shoots of the tall *Aster novae-angliae*.

The day lilies rapidly recovered and have gone on to a perfectly satisfactory summer, but the asters were set back so that few stalks have set flower buds this fall. Individual chicken-wire cages weren't a defense, because the woodchucks stood upright against the cages, bent them down and stripped the leaves from the wounded stems yet another time.

Lily bulbs were a casualty of smaller rodents. Or the woodchuck family might have wanted to vary its diet.

Deer have become a familiar sight on our property which is just one mile from downtown New London. One side of our property borders natural areas of the Connecticut Arboretum and it is here that deer have made their trails for trespass. As the unmanaged natural areas grow up to woodland from the fields they once were, the deer migrate to the less shady margins where there is a shrubby ecotone—in this case—my

garden. Their target was a new planting of several cultivars of Southern white cedar, especially *Chamaecyparis thyoides* 'Andelyensis.' This took cruel abuse, with all the branchlets stripped from one side of the plant, right to the center stem, and the growing tip itself crushed off in the typical fashion of the blunt-cut deer browse damage. The spreading English yew which had grown over fifteen years to a magnificent specimen ten feet across and four feet high had every growing tip stripped and crushed. Recovery has been slow, and the sight of stubby tufts of short needles along the branches puts one in mind of witches-broom plants.

Recent studies on controlling deer damage have not been encouraging, because when the animals are hungry, they will eat anything. Since there can be no retribution by hunting where houses are close together, or where dwellings are as close as 200 yards, fencing is the only recourse. When one lives at the edge of a natural area, it would be difficult to protect plantings with a fence higher than 6 feet (which they can jump). So, the yew will be but a memory next year. The cedar cultivar might be defended by an individual fence or cage around it, but what a way to garden!

The deer population of Connecticut is larger than in the days of early Colonial settlement because sentiment tends to create an extension of the "Bambi syndrome." With the cost of fish approaching $10.00 a pound, venison harvesting by skilled hunters would not be sacrilege. The demise of the English yew has hardened my heart. 🦋

Nests often hidden by foliage become apparent when the leaves fall.

Photo by F.B. Grunzweig
The National Audubon Society Collection
(Photo Researchers, Inc.)

Selected References:

Books

Davison, Verne E. *Attracting Birds from the Prairies to the Atlantic.* Thomas Crowell Co., New York. 1967.

A guide to the favorite foods, nesting sites and water needs of 400 species of migratory birds, as well as a separate section on plants for food, arranged by common name. 252 pp.

De Graf, Richard M. and Witmer, Gretchen M. *Trees, Shrubs and Vines for Attracting Birds.* U. of Mass. Press, Amherst. 1979.

Native trees and shrubs are beautifully illustrated with black and white drawings. Text covers descriptions of flowers, fruits, leaves, habitat and landscape notes. A classic. 194 pp.

Dennis, John V. *The Wildlife Gardener.* Alfred Knopf, New York. 1985.

A complete discussion of wildlife and their garden habitats, including misunderstood reptiles and amphibians, mammals, insects beneficial and non-beneficial, earthworms, and birds. The black and white illustrations are fine, increasing the appeal of an unusually well presented book. 293 pp.

Kress, Stephen. *The Audubon Society Guide to Attracting Birds.* Alfred Knopf, New York. 1986.

Contains tables of recommended trees, shrubs and flowering plants for all of North America; plans for gardens, pools, ponds, feeding stations, diagrams for birdhouses, hints from birders around the country.

Pamphlets

Shrubs and Vines for Northeastern Wildlife. Northeastern Forest Experiment Station, Upper Darby, Pa. USDA Forest Service General Technical Report NE-9 1974.

A manual which describes 40 native shrubs, vines, and trees; their life history and use by wildlife; how to propagate and manage.

Planning for Wildlife in Cities and Suburbs. Fish and Wildlife Service, U.S. Department of the Interior. Superintendent of Documents, U.S. Government Printing Office, Washington, D.C. 20402. Stock Number 024-010-00471-1. 1978.

The booklet was prepared in conjunction with the American Society of Planning Officials and explores the importance of site design, habitat types, and the integration of wildlife considerations into site designs, vegetation management of open spaces along highways, airports as well as backyards of urban settlements.

Periodicals

The Living Bird. A quarterly publication of the Laboratory of Ornithology, Cornell University. 150 Sapsucker Woods Road, Ithaca, N.Y. 14850.

The Audubon Society's Video Guide to the Birds of North America: I.

A new series of video cassettes, now present four two-hour tapes covering all the North American breeding birds. The first tape features loons, grebes, pelicans, waterfowl, hawks. Behavior while diving, feeding, playing and flying is shown. Bird calls, verbal descriptions and animated range maps depicting migration routes are all part of this exciting package. Available from The Crow's Nest Bookshop, Laboratory of Ornithology, Cornell University, Sapsucker Woods Road, Ithaca, New York, 14850 for about $70.00

Other Publications

Bell, W. J. And R. T. Carde, editors. 1984. Chemical Ecology of Insects. Sinauer Associates, Inc. Sunderland, Massachusetts.

Brower, L. P. Ecological Chemistry. Scientific American, February 1969.

Erlich, P. R. and P. H. Raven. Butterflies and Plants. Scientific American, June 1967.

Wallace, J. W. and R. L. Mansell, editors. 1976. Biochemical Interaction Between Plants and Insects. Recent Advances in Phytochemistry, Vol. 10.